English for academic study:

Listening

D0565509

Course Book

Colin Campbell and Jonathan Smith

University of Reading

CALS
Centre for
Applied Language Studies

Garnet EDUCATION

Credits

Acknowledgements

Published by
Garnet Publishing Ltd.
8 Southern Court
South Street
Reading RG1 4QS, UK

ISBN: 978 1 85964 538 3

A catalogue record for this book is available from The Library of Congress.

Production
Project manager: Simone Davies
Project consultant: Rod Webb
Editorial team: Penny Analytis, Jo Caulkett,
                      Emily Clarke, Chris Gough, Fiona McGarry
American English
adaptation: Jennifer Allen, Arley Gray
Art director: Mike Hinks
Design and layout: Sarah Church, Neil Collier
Photography: Corbis
Audio: Paul Rubens Productions, New York

The mind map on page 34 appears courtesy of www.learningfundamentals.com.au

Every effort has been made to trace copyright holders and we apologize in advance for any unintentional omissions. We will be happy to insert the appropriate acknowledgements in any subsequent editions.

Printed and bound in Lebanon by International Press.

A large number of people contributed in different ways to the production of this book, although all responsibility for any mistakes remains ours alone.

We would like to thank the following for their permission to use extracts from the lectures that were originally recorded as part of the British Academic Spoken English (BASE) corpus:

Professor Michael Utton, Professor Alan Roberts (Rennes Business School, France), Dr Steve Wiggins, Alan Rowley, Dr Clare Furneaux, Dr Elizabeth Gaffan, Dr Colin Beardsley, Professor Peter Roach and Dr Rupert Loader.

In addition we would like to thank Shelagh Tonkyn for permission to use an extract from a lecture on Magistrates' Courts given at the University of Reading, and acknowledge the influence of the ideas of Beverly Fairfax on features of lecture introductions in Unit 2, and those of Tony Lynch on ideas on note-taking in Unit 4 of this book.

Our colleagues, Dr Paul Thompson and Sarah Creer, were very helpful in making the BASE corpus available and accessible to us, and in suggesting suitable lectures from the corpus.

The following colleagues gave invaluable feedback on parts of this book, and their contribution is gratefully acknowledged: Emma Grenside, Bruce Howell, Anne Pallant, John Slaght, Lucy Watson and Sebastian Watkins. We would also like to thank Nicola Taylor and her in-sessional students for giving us the opportunity to trial some of the material in the book.

Colin Campbell and Jonathan Smith, Authors, April 2009, Centre for Applied Language Studies, University of Reading, UK.

Contents

Book Map

	Topic	Skills focus	Micro-skills
1	• Language and Linguistics • Academic Culture	• Listening in different languages • Issues in understanding spoken English • Listening to lectures	—
2	• Migration • Britain and European Monetary Union • Globalization • District Courts	• Thinking about introductions • Functions and language of lecture introductions • Listening to lecture introductions	Word stress
3	• Franchising	• Thinking about key ideas • Identifying key points in a lecture • Distinguishing key points from examples • Signposting key points	Word families (1)
4	• America's Transport Systems • The East-Asian Miracle	• Reasons for taking notes • Principles of note-taking • Note-taking practice	Understanding sentence stress
5	• Purposes of Education • World Economy • Health in the United States	• Returning to your notes • Using abbreviations and symbols • Organizing your notes	Word boundaries
6	• Embedded words • European Union: regulations and directives • Market Dominance and Monopoly	• Introducing new terminology • Lecture 1: Embedded words • Lecture 2: Introducing terms and concepts (1) • Lecture 3: Introducing terms and concepts (2)	Weak forms of function words
7	• Doing Market Research • Social Learning • Contestable Markets	• Macro-structure of lectures	Word families (2)
8	• Social Learning • Market Research • Integrated Rural Development	• Identifying digressions	Common expressions in lectures

Introduction

This book has been designed with two main purposes in mind:
- to help you better understand spoken English, particularly the spoken English of academic lectures;
- to help you develop your note-taking skills while listening.

1. Audio recordings

Many of the lecture extracts in this book are based on transcripts of actual lectures given to students as part of their normal degree programs. Although the extracts have been re-recorded to ensure clarity, the language and most of the content of these lectures have been maintained, to ensure that you are provided with listening practice that closely simulates listening to and taking notes from real academic lectures.

The lecture extracts are taken from a range of academic fields, including investment banking, development economics, marketing, psychology, and linguistics. Although the original lectures were intended for students majoring in these subjects, we have chosen extracts that should be accessible to a general audience of students.

Other extracts have been written especially for this book, but have also been designed to reflect features of actual academic lectures.

The recordings are available on audio CD.

2. Structure of the book

Apart from the first unit, all the units are divided into two sections; macro-skills and micro-skills.

Macro-skills include such things as:
- using lecture introductions;
- note-taking;
- recognizing the structure of lectures.

Micro-skills focus on linguistic features of spoken English such as:
- recognizing words that are spoken quickly and are not stressed;
- recognizing where one spoken word ends and the next begins;
- word stress and sentence stress.

In these units you will also find items called *Sound advice*, which either summarize key points from the unit or give advice on listening strategies.

At the end of the book you will find transcripts for all the lectures in the book. Your instructor will ask you to look at these transcripts and occasionally, after you have completed the main listening tasks, give you the opportunity to listen to the recording and follow the transcript at the same time. Doing this will help you learn the spoken forms of words that you may only know in their written form.

3. Vocabulary

Although the recordings in the book may not be related to your particular subject, you will find a lot of useful vocabulary in this book.

There are different types of vocabulary that you may find useful:
- academic words—these are words that occur frequently in many different academic subjects, so whatever you are studying, it is important to learn how to use these words;

- non-technical topic words—many of the recordings use sets of topic vocabulary that will be useful to students regardless of their major; for example, the text on market research contains many words connected with surveys and questionnaires and statistics;

- subject-specific words—some of the recordings contain words that will be of particular interest to students of specific subjects. For example, there is an extract on social learning that will be of particular interest to students planning to study psychology.

4. Listening outside the classroom

Your listening will improve more quickly if you practice outside the classroom. You can do this in a variety of ways, for example, talking with English-speaking friends, listening to the radio or watching TV, or working with independent study materials.

You will find *Sound advice* sections in most units in this book, and these contain useful advice for improving your listening. Here are some more ideas.

- There are a number of good websites that provide practice in listening to academic lectures. If you go to the EAS website (enter through http://www.englishforacademicstudy.com) you will find links to these sites.

- A wide range of vocabulary is part of the key to success in listening. You should keep a record of new words or phrases that you meet, and you should make sure you write down the pronunciation, particularly if it does not fit in with pronunciation patterns you are familiar with. Ask the instructor to model the pronunciation if you are not sure of it.

- There are several dictionaries on CD-ROM on which you can hear the pronunciation (and see the meaning) of a word on screen, either by moving the mouse pointer over a word or by clicking on it. Think about buying one because it will be useful, not just on this course, but in your later studies.

1 Listening and Lectures

In this unit you will:
- discuss the different situations in which you have to listen;
- identify what factors influence your ability to understand;
- learn about features of lectures in different academic cultures.

Task 1: Listening in different languages

With a partner or in groups, discuss the following questions.

a) In your own language, which of these types of listening do you think is more difficult or requires more attention? Why?

- listening to friends as part of your conversation with them;
- listening to the radio;
- listening to announcements at a crowded bus station;
- listening to an academic lecture.

b) What experiences have you had of listening to spoken English?

c) What type of listening in English do you find more demanding/less demanding?

Task 2: Issues in understanding spoken English

2.1 **Look at the following factors that make it difficult to listen to and understand spoken English. With a partner, add two or three more factors to this list.**

- the speed at which someone is speaking;

- background noise;

- _____

- _____

- _____

2.2 **CD1 – 1 Listen to Part 1 of a talk in which a professor describes some of the problems of listening. Then answer the following questions.**

a) Which of the factors in Ex 2.1 did she talk about?

b) Which other factors did she talk about?

c) After talking about the factors that affect listening, the professor discusses two additional problems that students may have. What are they?

2.3 ⊕ CD1 – 2 **Now listen to Part 2 of the talk, in which the professor illustrates the two problems she has introduced. The professor asks you to write down a phrase. Do this as you listen.**

_____

Does this example make the points clearer?

2.4 ⊕ CD1 – 3 **Listen to Part 3 of the talk. Complete this excerpt by writing two to six words in each blank.**

> So what is the solution to these two problems? Well, first you need to get as much practice listening to natural speech as possible. Listen to _____ and try to develop your understanding of how words and phrases are really pronounced, not how you _____ pronounced. Secondly, you _____ that when you listen you may misunderstand what is being said. So you need to be ready to _____ about your understanding of the meaning, if what you hear _____ compared to what you understood before. And this means taking a flexible, open-minded approach to listening.

2.5 **Reflect on the talk you just listened to in Ex 2.2 – 2.4. Answer the following questions.**

a) Did you have any difficulties doing this activity?

b) If so, why do you think you had problems?

c) Were they the same problems the professor talked about?

Task 3: Listening to lectures

You are going to listen to a professor talking about the differences he perceives between lectures in the US and in China.

3.1 **With a partner, discuss your experiences of lectures in your own country and/or in the country where you are studying. Think about the following.**

- what the professors did, e.g., _read from notes, used visuals, asked questions_, etc.
- what the students did, e.g., _asked questions, took notes_, etc.

3.2 In Part 1 of the talk, the professor describes the following:

- what his main interest is;
- where he got his information about lectures in China;
- the survey he did and the students he talked to.

⊕ CD1 – 4 **Listen to Part 1 of the talk and make notes about the above points.**

3.3 With a partner, compare your notes for Ex 3.2. Then answer the following questions.

a) Did you record the same information?

b) Could you have recorded the information in different ways using fewer words/different words? How?

3.4 ⊙ CD1 – 5 In Part 2 of the talk, the professor first talks about some of the characteristics of lectures in China and then compares these with lectures in the US.
Listen and make notes on the main points he makes.

China	US

3.5 With a partner, compare your notes for Ex 3.4. Then answer the following questions.

a) Did you record the same information?

b) Could you have recorded the information in different ways, using fewer words/different words? How?

3.6 Now, respond to the talk. In groups, look at the following questions and discuss your reactions to what the professor said in Ex 3.2 and 3.4.

a) If you are from China, do you agree with what the speaker reported about lectures in China?

b) If you are from another country, are the lectures in your country more like the American system, the Chinese one, or a combination of both?

c) Have you already listened to lectures in English?

d) Did you take notes (in English or your own language) during the lectures you have attended?

e) Was it difficult to take notes? If so, why?

f) What did you do before and after your lectures to help you understand more fully and remember the content?

Unit summary

In this unit you have discussed the different situations in which you have to listen. You have also identified the factors that influence your ability to understand, and learned about features of lectures in different academic cultures.

1 **Look at the listening issues below and decide in which circumstances they affect you. Choose from one of the circumstances below and mark F, L, R or A in the first box.**

F—This affects me when I speak to English-speaking friends.
L—This affects me when I listen to lectures.
R—This affects me when I listen to the radio or watch TV.
A—This affects me if I listen to announcements.

a) You are concentrating on something else at the same time as you listen.

b) You are nervous because missing something important will have a negative consequence.

c) The speaker is using lots of words and phrases that you don't know.

d) The speaker speaks very quickly and runs words together. Even common words are difficult to catch.

e) The speaker does not do or say things in the way that somebody in your country would.

f) The speaker is talking about a topic you know nothing about.

g) The speaker is using a lot of specialized vocabulary.

h) Other people interrupt the speaker so you can't follow the flow.

i) The speaker doesn't tell you when you should listen especially carefully.

j) There is a lot of background noise.

2 **Now look again at each issue and decide whether it is a problem for you or not. In the second box, mark P if it is a problem and you need to practice or N if it is not a problem.**

3 **Which of the issues did the speaker in the unit offer solutions to?**

For web resources relevant to this unit, see:
www.englishforacademicstudy.com/us/student/listening/links

2 Introductions to Lectures

In this unit you will:
- look at how a lecture introduction can help you to understand the lecture better;
- practice making notes on introductions to lectures;
- learn how to recognize words that may be pronounced differently to the way you expect them to be.

Task 1: Thinking about introductions

1.1 What do you expect the professor to talk about in the introduction to a lecture?

1.2 Think of lectures you have heard. Did the professors try to make the structure of the lecture obvious to students? If so, how?

1.3 Two students took notes on the introduction to a lecture about migration. Look at the notes they took. How are the notes different?

Student 1:

> Migration from Arab world, e.g., Syria/Jordan — effect on US security, etc.

Student 2:

> Not migration from Arab world BUT internal US migration, e.g., country → city

1.4 ⊙ CD1 – 6 **Listen to the introduction. Then answer the following questions.**

a) Which student understood what the professor was going to talk about?

b) Why do you think the other student made a mistake?

c) Which words in the introduction signal what the professor will talk about?

Sound advice: In an introduction, the speaker may define the scope of the lecture by explaining what will *not* be discussed, as well as what *will* be discussed.

Read the items in the left-hand column of the table (What professors do in introductions).

a) Check (✓) the items you discussed in Ex 1.1 and 1.2. Make sure you understand what the other items mean.

b) Match the items from the left-hand column to the statements in the right-hand column.

What professors do in introductions	Professor statements
a) limit the scope of the lecture; in other words, say what they will talk about and what they will not talk about	**1** There are in a sense two themes—there's a qualitative stream of market research, and there's a quantitative stream. I'm going to deal with basically the quantitative stream of data collection first.
b) comment on a theory they have just described	**2** However, that's not the type of migration I want to look at today. What I want to look at is internal migration, i.e., the movement of people from country to city, and vice versa, and from one city to another.
c) preview the content or structure of the current lecture	**3** Sara Shettleworth has a superb chapter on social learning, and I'm going to mention just a few of the examples that she mentions.
d) refer to research on the subject—this often includes mentioning specific reading material	**4** What I want to do first is just to, because I know some of you are not familiar with the EU, is just give a very simple introduction to European Union institutions.
e) give background information on the lecture topic	**5** I undertook a study in the mid eighties, and it was quite easy for me to find 22 markets.
f) introduce different approaches to the subject	**6** I'll be giving you a handout with these quotes, so you don't have to write them down verbatim.
g) refer to what students should/should not write down	**7** My critique about the theory of perfect contestability is that if you change the assumptions slightly, the predictions change dramatically. It's very unstable.
h) indicate that they are referring back to previous lectures and remind students of the content of those lectures	**8** Last semester we looked at how accounting systems were different. We looked at France and Germany and the Netherlands, and so forth, to see how the financial reports are different.
i) explain the professor's own interest in the subject, for example, any research they have done	**9** So today's session—I'm going to talk about the local environment, the role of local government, and also look at the interaction with the community.

Note: The left-hand column shows what professors commonly do in introductions to lectures. All the statements in the right-hand column are from introductions to lectures.

Task 3: Listening to lecture introductions

You are going to listen to the introductions to three different lectures. Before you listen to each introduction, you will do some activities to help you anticipate the content of the lectures.

3.1 **The first lecture is entitled *Britain and the European Monetary Union*. Before you listen, discuss the following questions with a partner.**

a) What is the EMU?

b) Is Britain a member of the EMU?

c) What do you think is Britain's attitude to the EU? And to the US?

Make sure you understand the following phrases from the lecture.

single currency	opt out	the Commonwealth	Eurozone

3.2 CD1 – 7 **Listen to the introduction to the lecture *Britain and the European Monetary Union*. Which aspects from the checklist in Task 2 does the professor use?**

3.3 **The second lecture is entitled *Globalization*. Before you listen, discuss the following questions with a partner.**

a) What does *globalization* mean to you?

b) What kind of people does it affect?

c) Which department of the university do you think the professor will be from?

Make sure you understand the following words and phrases from the lecture.

stockbrokers	global tycoons	sociologist	implications

3.4 CD1 – 8 **Listen to the introduction to the lecture *Globalization*. Which aspects from the checklist in Task 2 does the professor use?**

3.5 **The third lecture is entitled *District Courts*. Before you listen, discuss the following questions with a partner.**

a) How many different types of courts do you have in your country?

b) What problems do the different courts deal with?

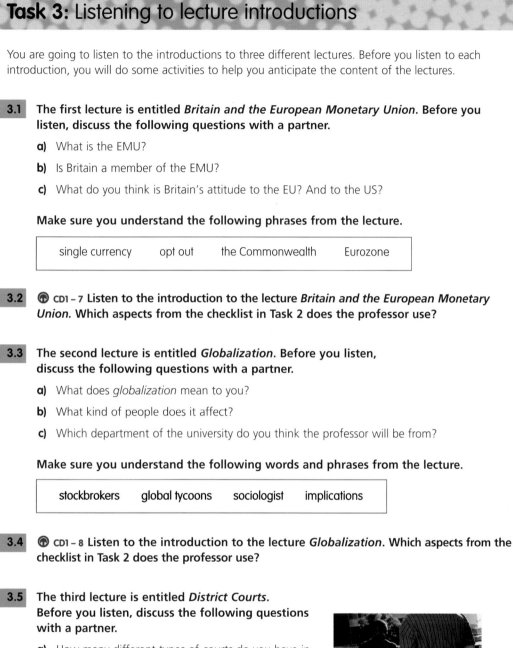

Make sure you understand the following phrases from the lecture.

non-criminal matters	maintenance of children	criminal offenses

3.6 CD1 – 9 **Listen to the introduction to the lecture _District Courts_. Which aspects from the checklist in Task 2 does the professor use?**

Note: At the beginning of the lecture the speaker refers to "John," the person who has introduced her.

Sound advice: Listen carefully to the introductions to all your lectures. Doing so may help you to understand the lectures better and take better notes.

Task 4: Micro-skills: Word stress

4.1 CD1 – 10 **Listen and complete the sentence from the introduction to _Britain and the European Monetary Union_.**

> However, _____,
> I'm going to spend most of the time today talking about
> why Britain _____ the
> euro, and then about whether I think Britain might join
> the Eurozone in the future and in what circumstances.

Study tip

You may not recognize the spoken forms of words, although you might easily understand them when reading. This is partly because words are sometimes not pronounced in the way you expect them to be.

Answer the following questions.

a) Were the missing words ones you already knew?

b) If you already knew the words, did you recognize them when you heard them? If you didn't, why didn't you recognize them?

Sound advice: A better understanding of the reality behind the pronunciation of English will help you develop your listening skills. One aspect of pronunciation that may cause difficulties in listening is the issue of word stress and its influence on the pronunciation of vowel sounds. For example, you may not have recognized _adopted_ in Ex 4.1, either because you expected a different pronunciation or because you did not hear the initial /ə/.

4.2 CD1 – 11 **Listen and complete the following sentences from the introduction to _District Courts_. Write one word in each blank.**

> So, for example, in the case of family breakup, it would involve making parental
> _____ orders where the parents can't agree on how much _____ time
> each parent should have with the child.
>
> What we're mainly _____ with today is criminal offenses, and that's
> what I'm going to spend most of my time talking about this morning.

Answer the following questions.

a) How do you pronounce the words you have written?

b) The first syllable of each word is spelled the same, but in the second extract it is pronounced differently. Why?

4.3 **Put the words in the box into the correct column according to their stress pattern.**

~~access~~	~~account~~	adapt	aspect	assist	assume
connect	consist	consume	contact	context	control
process (n)	produce (v)	product	promise	protect	provide

O o	o O
access	account

a) Now label the words in the two columns *adjective* (adj), *noun* (n) or *verb* (v).

b) Look at where the stress falls in two-syllable words. Can you see a connection between word form and word stress in two-syllable words?

4.4 CD1 – 12 **Listen to a recording about security and computers. Complete the text with one word in each blank. Use words from Ex 4.3.**

Security is an important _____ of using a computer that many people don't pay much attention to. If you buy a laptop or personal computer, you'll probably want to _____ to the Internet. If so, it's important that you install security software that'll protect it from attack by viruses or spyware. Now there is a wide range of _____ available on the market that are relatively cheap and that _____ a variety of different features. For example, in addition to checking their computer for viruses, parents can use the software to _____ which websites their children can _____. You shouldn't _____, however, that you are 100 percent safe if you're using such security software. You should make sure that you have backup copies of your work, and you should be very careful about keeping important information, such as bank _____ details, on your computer.

4.5 CD1 – 13 **Listen to a recording about competition between large supermarket chains and small local shops in the UK. Complete the text with one word in each blank. All the words begin with *con~*, *pro~* or *a~*.**

As in the United States, supermarket chains in the UK are always looking for new opportunities. Because of planning restrictions, the large UK chains are currently looking to expand their businesses and increase _____ by opening smaller "convenience stores." Organizations representing small, independent shops _____ that they now face unfair competition from the large chains. And they _____ the large chains of a number of practices that make it difficult for them to compete. First, it's _____ that below-cost pricing is used by large supermarkets to force smaller, local shops out of business. Second, the large chains often buy up land that is not immediately used, and this prevents smaller local businesses from entering the market.

There is also some _____ that the large chains are treating UK suppliers unfairly. Farmers claim that they are being paid less for their products, and are reluctant to complain for fear of losing key _____. However, supermarkets argue that the _____ is the best regulator of the market.

Look at the words you have written in the blanks. Does the stress fall on the first or second syllable? How do you pronounce these words?

4.6 **Put the words in the box into the correct column according to their stress pattern.**

decent	decide	decline	defend	delay	dentist
effect	emerge	equal	even	event	expert	extinct
reflect	rely	report	reptile	rescue

O o	o O
decent	decide

4.7 CD1 – 14 **Listen to a recording about the effect of global warming on numbers of polar bears. Complete the text with one word in each blank. Use words from Ex 4.6.**

Wildlife _____ predict that numbers of polar bears will _____ by at least 50 percent over the next 50 years because of global warming. Polar bears _____ on sea ice to catch seals for food, and it's _____ that ice floes in the Arctic are disappearing at an alarming rate. Scientists _____ that the animals are already beginning to suffer the _____ of climate change in some parts of Canada, and if there is any further _____ in tackling this problem, polar bears may be _____ by the end of the century.

4.8 CD1 – 15 **Listen to a recording about monitoring water levels in rivers. Complete the text with one word in each blank. All the words begin with de~, re~, or e~.**

Scientists are now able to monitor river levels using information from satellites by using a computer program _____ by researchers at De Montfort University in Leicester in the UK. Satellites have been able to measure the height of the sea by timing how long it takes to _____ a beam bounced back off waves. But until now, interference from objects on the banks of rivers has made it impossible to measure river levels.

However, the new program, which is based on data collected over the last _____, is specially _____ to filter out this interference. This new technology will be particularly useful in monitoring river levels in _____ areas. It will, for example, enable scientists to _____ river level patterns over the _____ Amazon river basin, contributing towards our understanding of climate change.

Look at the words you have written in the blanks. Does the stress fall on the first or second syllable? How do you pronounce these words?

Unit summary

In this unit you have seen how a lecture introduction can help you to better understand the lecture and practiced taking notes on introductions to lectures. You have also focused on words that may be pronounced differently from the way you expect them to be.

1 **Look at these extracts from lecture introductions. Underline the topic of each lecture.**

a) Now, you may think that a lecture entitled *Britain and the European Monetary Union* will be about Britain's plans to join the EMU, but what we will actually look at today is why Britain is not part of the monetary union.

b) What I especially want to focus on today is low-paid employment within the public sector, and not get sidetracked into talking about the many underpaid individuals in the private sector or indeed the unemployed.

c) Rather than talk at length about crime figures as a whole, I'm going to concentrate on crime that is considered to be drug-related. That means crime that occurs because the perpetrator needs to buy drugs to satisfy an addiction; crimes like burglary and common theft, for example.

2 **Complete each of these approaches to lecture introductions with a word from below.**

theory	interest	background	scope	previous
	approaches	research	content	

a) limit the _____ of the lecture

b) comment on a _____

c) preview the _____ or structure of the current lecture

d) refer to _____ that has been done into the subject

e) give _____ information to the lecture topic

f) introduce different _____ to the subject

g) indicate that they are referring back to _____ lectures

h) explain the professor's own _____ in the subject

> For web resources relevant to this unit, see:
> **www.englishforacademicstudy.com/us/student/listening/links**

3 Identifying Key Ideas in Lectures

In this unit you will:
- practice identifying the key points a professor wants to make;
- distinguish key points from examples;
- use your understanding of examples to deduce key points;
- develop your understanding of relationships between ideas;
- learn patterns of pronunciation and word stress in word families.

Task 1: Thinking about key ideas

With a partner or in groups, discuss the following questions.

a) Why is it important to recognize key ideas (or main points) in a lecture?

b) Why do professors use examples?

Task 2: Identifying key points in a lecture

2.1 **You are going to listen to the first part of a lecture on franchising. Before you listen, discuss the following questions with a partner.**

a) What is franchising?

b) Can you think of any businesses that are run as franchises?

2.2 🎧 CD1 – 16 **Listen to Part 1 of the lecture, which is in three sections. Identify the three sections from the following list and put them in the correct order.**

☐ a definition of franchising

☐ examples of successful franchises

☐ one reason for setting up a franchise business

☐ how franchising works

☐ the types of business that are suitable for franchising

2.3 🎧 CD1 – 17 **Listen to Part 1 Section 1 again and answer the following questions.**

a) Why does the professor talk about hairdressing salons?

b) Look at the following points the professor makes in Section 1. Which is the key idea in this section? What is the relationship between the key idea and the other points?

- You may need large amounts of money or to bring in new skills to expand your business.

- As a business expands, the owner will not have the same amount of personal control over the operation of the business as he used to.

- As successful businesses develop, they often reach a stage when expansion brings risks.

- You can minimize the risks of developing your business by franchising it.

2.4 🎧 CD1 – 18 **Listen to Part 1 Section 2 again. In pairs, discuss what the following terms mean in the context of the lecture.**

franchisor	franchisee	trademark	trade name
package	untrained person	continual assistance	

2.5 🎧 CD1 – 19 **Listen to Part 1 Section 3 again.**

a) What does the franchisor provide to the franchisee?

b) What does the franchisee give in return?

Task 3: Distinguishing key points from examples

The professor begins Part 2 of the lecture by saying: "There are a number of issues that you need to consider when deciding whether or not to franchise your business."

3.1 **With a partner, discuss what you think the professor will talk about in Part 2 of the lecture.**

3.2 🎧 CD1 – 20 **Listen to Part 2 of the lecture.**

a) Make brief notes in your notebook on the three or four points made by the professor, maximum 15 words for each point.

b) Compare your notes with a partner and see whether you have identified the same points.

3.3 **Look at the transcript for Track 20 on page 68 and find examples of language used by the professor to signpost key points.**

For example, the professor signposts the first point by saying:
"First, there needs to be …"

3.4 🎧 CD1 – 21/22 **Listen to Part 2 Sections 1 and 2 again and answer the following questions.**

Section 1

a) To support his key point, the professor gives two reasons and two examples. What are they?

b) Do they help make his point clearer? If so, how?

Section 2

a) What point does the professor make about buying supplies in bulk?

b) How is this point related to the key point in this section?

c) Now look at the text on the next page. Having made the key point, the speaker repeats the idea twice. Underline the words where he repeats the idea.

In addition—and this is fairly obvious—you will need a fairly wide margin between cost and income. Remember that the gross margin needs to provide a return on the investment to both the franchisor and the franchisee. So you will need to keep costs low and prices as high as the market will bear. One advantage of a franchise operation is that supplies can be bought in bulk across the whole franchise, which will help to keep costs down. But you can see that franchising would be unsuitable in a market where the margin between cost and income is very narrow.

3.5 ☞ CD1 – 23 **Listen to Part 2 Section 3 again, where the professor talks about training and support, the operating manual, and developing skills quickly.**

a) How are the above three ideas related to one another?

b) What point does the professor make about previous experience?

Task 4: Signposting key points

In Part 3, the professor continues to discuss some of the issues that need to be considered when trying to decide whether or not to franchise your business.

4.1 ☞ CD1 – 24 **Listen to Part 3 of the lecture. Make notes on the key points in your notebook. Then compare your notes with a partner. Have you identified the same key points?**

4.2 ☞ CD1 – 25 **Listen to Part 3 Section 1 again and complete the excerpt with one to three words in each blank.**

Note: Notice that again the professor uses signposting language to indicate he is beginning a new point.

> One further issue you may need to consider is whether the business is _____ to another geographical area. If you have developed your business serving one particular part of the country and you want to set up a franchise network covering a _____, the whole country, for example, another thing you will have to consider is whether there is a _____ for your product or service in different regions. It may be, for example, that competition in other parts of the country may be so _____ that it is difficult for franchisees to _____, or that for localized _____ or _____ reasons the business may not be as profitable.

Study tip

A technique often used by professors to highlight ideas is to stress key words or phrases. Trying to identify where the speaker does this can help you recognize key points in a lecture.

4.3 ☞ CD1 – 26/27 **Listen to Part 3 Sections 2 and 3 again. Make notes on the different ways in which brands can be protected.**

a) Underline the signposting language used to highlight key points.

b) 🎧 **CD1 – 26/27** Now listen again and circle any key words or phrases the professor stresses.

Note: You may also notice that the speaker sometimes pauses after key points.

Finally, when you are setting up a franchise network, you will need to bear in mind that you will be losing direct control of the way your brand is perceived by the customer, so this brings me to my last point, which is to emphasize the importance of protecting your brand. I am sure you are all aware that it often takes a long time to establish a distinctive brand with a valuable reputation, but that this reputation can be damaged comparatively quickly if, for example, quality standards are not consistently applied. The detailed operating manual that I referred to earlier will play a role in maintaining the brand but, just as important, you need to take care selecting franchisees and monitoring their operations. In addition to checking that franchisees have the relevant skills and experience to run a successful business, you also need to ensure that they share the same business values as you, that they accept the importance of maintaining the brand and that they are clear about what they can or can't change about the way the business is run—so people who are very individualistic will probably not make good franchisees.

The written agreement between the franchisor and the franchisee should specify very clearly what performance and quality standards are expected, and much of the initial training will be ensuring that staff have the skills to achieve these standards. However, regular visits to franchise units are essential in ensuring that the standards are being applied consistently and uniformly, and ongoing training may be necessary to deal with issues that are uncovered in these visits. Protecting the brand is ultimately in the interests of both the franchisor and the franchisee, because for the franchisee one of the main advantages of running a franchise is that they are buying into and helping to consolidate an established brand.

Sound advice:

- As you listen, try to keep in mind the key ideas and relate any new information you hear to those ideas.
- Listen for signposting language, stressed words or phrases and pauses, as indicators of key points.
- If you do not understand a key point, listen for any examples that may help you to recover the meaning.

Task 5: Micro-skills: Word families (1)

You can extend your vocabulary by learning groups of words that have the same basic form and that are often related in meaning.

Examples:

Noun	Verb	Adjective
pr<u>o</u>duct, production, productivity	pro<u>duce</u>	productive
definition	define	definite, definitive
economy, economics, economist	economize	economic, economical

5.1 **Practice the pronunciation of the words in the table and underline the stressed syllable in each word.**

5.2 **Use the words in the table to study how changes in syllable stress within word families affect pronunciation.**

In many cases, a different syllable stress has an effect on the pronunciation of the sounds.

Example:
pr<u>o</u>duct   /ˈprɒdʌkt/
pro<u>duce</u>   /prəˈdjuːs/

5.3 ⊕ CD1 – 28 **You can also modify the meaning of a word by adding a prefix, for example, *interpret/misinterpret, assess/reassess, appear/disappear*. Listen to the following sentences and write in the missing prefix to each word.**

How do the prefixes change the meaning of the original words?

a) All unions were declared _____legal by the government.

b) This is one example of a _____match between the individual's goals and those of the organization.

c) They found no significant _____relation between class size and levels of achievement.

d) Real estate _____actions rose by 30 percent last month.

e) Prices are determined through the _____action of supply and demand.

f) These animals exhibited _____normal behavior compared to the control group.

5.4 ⊕ CD1 – 29 **Listen to the following sentences and complete them with two to four words in each blank. Some of the words include prefixes.**

a) We had to get _____, because the detail was not very clear on the original ones.

b) Many doctors work _____, which puts them under a lot of stress.

c) Crime prevention is _____ of the police's work, but it is often difficult to assess its effectiveness.

d) Doctors have noticed _____, such as bulimia and anorexia, not just among young women but, surprisingly, among young men.

> **Study tip**
>
> If you think about the grammar *and* meaning of each sentence as you do the exercise, you are more likely to get the correct answers.

e) These plants should be grown in partial shade, rather than _____ .

f) Researchers have found that _____ much more likely to be involved in traffic accidents.

5.5 🎧 **CD1 – 30** **Listen to the following groups of sentences. Complete the sentences with two to four words in each blank. One of the words in each blank is a form of the word in bold.**

a) Children need a **secure** environment in which to grow up.

Many immigrants are only able to find _____ .

The money was invested in _____ and property.

b) Achievement levels **vary** considerably from school to school in the city.

Some economists believe that interest rates can be predicted by examining

_____ .

In the UK's Eden Project, they have managed to create _____

of habitats.

There is _____ to health care in different

parts of the country.

c) How are we going to **solve** this problem?

You need to _____ in water before applying it to the crop.

There appears to be _____ between the two countries,

despite years of peace negotiations.

d) A mass spectrometer was used to **analyze** the gases.

_____ of the data is needed to confirm these initial findings.

The course is designed to help students to develop _____ .

e) The results **indicate** that the virus mutates more rapidly than was first believed.

All the _____ suggest that the economy is recovering.

The strike was _____ the level of the workers' frustration.

f) Chomsky was a fierce **critic** of Bush Senior's foreign policy.

There was _____ the way the election had been administered.

The negotiations _____ establishment of peace in the area.

Sound advice: Your listening skills will improve if you work to enlarge your vocabulary. Learning *word families* is an effective way of doing this, but you also need to develop your awareness of differences in pronunciation between words in each family. You can learn the most useful word families by referring to the Academic Word List and by doing the exercises in *EAS Vocabulary*.

Unit summary

In this unit you have practiced identifying key points in a lecture and seen how examples can help you understand a key point. You have also developed your understanding of relationships between ideas and learned patterns of pronunciation and word stress in word families.

1 **Which two statements about how a professor identifies key points in a lecture are not true? Mark each statement T (true) or F (false).**

a) The professor may use signposting words and phrases to indicate a key point.

b) The professor may use words and phrases that are specific to the topic of the lecture.

c) The professor may stress important words and phrases.

d) The professor may pause for a moment before introducing a key point.

e) The professor may repeat some key points.

f) The professor may speak very quickly at times to emphasize that a point is key.

g) The professor may give examples to support a key point.

h) The professor may give reasons why a point is important.

2 **Check the statement below that is true for you.**

a) I can now distinguish between key points and examples.

b) I still get confused about what the key point is and what an example is.

3 **When a professor uses typical words and phrases to indicate a key point, it is called "signposting." Write eight typical signposting words and phrases from the unit here.**

_____   _____

_____   _____

_____   _____

_____   _____

For web resources relevant to this unit, see:
www.englishforacademicstudy.com/us/student/listening/links

4 Note-taking: Part 1

In this unit you will:
- discuss the reasons for taking notes in a lecture;
- learn the principles of effective note-taking;
- practice taking notes from lectures.

Task 1: Reasons for taking notes

Discuss the following questions with a partner.

a) Why do students take notes in lectures?

b) What do they do with the notes after lectures?

c) Why will the volume and focus of the notes vary from one student to another?

d) When you are taking notes, what kind of information do you need to write down? What do you not need to write down?

Task 2: Principles of note-taking

2.1 **You are going to listen to an extract from a lecture on dealing with traffic problems in the US. Before you listen, discuss the following questions.**

a) Why do you think there are so many cars on the roads in the US?

b) What kind of problems does this create?

c) Can you think of any ways of reducing the amount of traffic? What are they?

2.2 🎧 CD1 – 31 **Listen to the recording and read the text at the same time.**

> So America's roads, and especially those in urban areas, are overcrowded. There are too many cars on the roads, and at particular times of the day and at particular places, traffic is either very slow or at a standstill. Now this has had a number of effects. First there is the economic effect, all the time wasted in traffic jams, which means a loss of productivity. Then there's the environmental effect. Cars produce a lot of pollution, which damages the local environment, but it also contributes to global warming. And there's also the effect on people's health. In addition to the poor air quality and the damage this causes to people's lungs, the stress of being stuck in traffic each day leads to a higher risk of heart disease.

2.3 Look at the following notes taken by a student during the lecture. Then answer the questions below.

> US roads overcrowded→ effects
>   – economic; loss of prod.vity
>   – environmental; pollution, glob. warming
>   – health probs.; lung, heart disease

a) Why has the student chosen this information to note down?

b) From your reading of the lecture extract, is there anything else the student should have written down?

c) Are the notes clear? When the student reads the notes a week later, will she be able to understand them?

d) What techniques did the student use to:
- make sure the notes are clear?
- save time?

2.4 Look at how this student has focused on the key ideas to produce her notes.

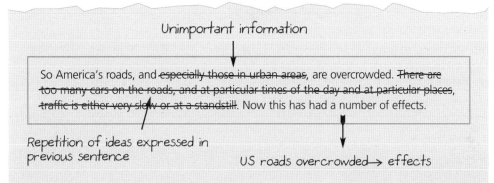

Unimportant information

So America's roads, and ~~especially those in urban areas~~, are overcrowded. ~~There are too many cars on the roads, and at particular times of the day and at particular places, traffic is either very slow or at a standstill~~. Now this has had a number of effects.

Repetition of ideas expressed in previous sentence

US roads overcrowded→ effects

2.5 What do you think the speaker will discuss in the rest of the lecture?

2.6 ⏺ CD1 – 32 Listen to Parts 2–4 of the lecture and continue the notes here. Before you listen, make sure you understand the meaning and pronunciation of the words in the boxes.

Part 2

Vocabulary | policy   measure (n)   integrated

Part 3

Vocabulary | consultation   investment |

Part 4

Vocabulary | (road) lane   CCTV   congestion |

Sound advice: When taking notes, you need to be:

- **selective:** decide what is important according to the speaker and according to your knowledge of the subject;
- **brief:** use abbreviations and symbols;
- **clear:** make sure the relationships between ideas are clearly related to each other.
  When you read the notes some time later, will you understand them?

Task 3: Note-taking practice

3.1   🎧 CD1 – 33 **Listen to Part 1 of an extract from a lecture on the history of development economics. The professor is discussing the reasons for rapid economic growth in East Asia in the 1980s.**

a) Before you listen, discuss these questions and make sure you understand the meaning and pronunciation of the vocabulary in the box.
- Which East Asian countries have developed rapidly since the 1980s?
- Can you explain the reasons for this rapid economic growth?

b) Listen to Part 1 and continue the notes in your notebook. Remember to be *selective*, *brief* and *clear*.

Part 1

Vocabulary | liberalism   intervention |

Interpreting East Asian economic miracle.
Dispute about influence of market liberalism,
e.g., China ...

3.2 🔊 CD1 – 34 In Part 2 of the extract, the professor goes on to discuss another factor. Listen to Part 2 and continue the notes.

Part 2

Vocabulary

| labor rates   stimulus |

Everyone agreed about one element ...

Task 4: Micro-skills: Understanding sentence stress

In Unit 3 you saw how *word* stress affects the pronunciation of syllables in the word. In a similar way, in any spoken *utterance*, certain words are stressed, and this affects the pronunciation of other words in the utterance.

4.1 🔊 CD1 – 35 Listen to this extract from Track 34. The main stressed syllables in this sentence are marked in bold.

> ..., that you could **always** hire a lot of people at **low** labor rates, but who were in reasonably good **health**, who were **literate** and who had reasonable **skills**.

Note: The speaker chooses to stress words that are particularly important to what he is saying. These tend to be *content words*, rather than function words.

One problem in listening is often that the *unstressed words* tend to be:
- pronounced in unexpected ways, e.g., *of* /əv/ and *but* /bət/;
- compressed together, so that it is difficult to hear where one word ends and another begins, e.g., *a lot of people* /əlɑːtəvpiːpəl/.

4.2 🔊 CD1 – 36 Listen to the following sentence from Track 33.

> The **Japanese** _____ **never** run _____ market **economy**.
> **Neither** _____ the **Koreans**.

a) Complete the sentences with one to three words in each blank.

b) The missing words are *function words* that are *unstressed*.
- How easy or difficult was it to hear these words?
- If it was difficult, could you work out what they were from the context?

4.3 Read the following extract from a lecture about market research. 🎧 CD1 – 37 Then listen to the extract and complete the sentences with two to seven words in each blank.

Note: The professor is making the point that when you are collecting market research data through a questionnaire, you need to test out the questionnaire on a small number of people to make sure it works well before you carry out the real survey.

You need to pre-test the questionnaire. This is really important. Those of you, some of you, will be doing this for your dissertation. Some of you, I know, _____

_____ .

You need to pre-test the thing, because you're the researcher. You're very

_____ . You know what you're talking about. But you've got to check that other people do as well. And if you want a statistically valid sample of a hundred people or two hundred people, then _____

_____ you're collecting the data properly. And it's here that these

_____ , they're going to tell you whether it's going to work or not.

So make sure that you do pilots, and, you know, this can be _____

_____ different people that you question.
I mean, you'll soon find out whether you've got any potential ... or any doubts about the length of the questionnaire, _____ , or
whether the sort of questions that you're asking are valid. You'll soon find out from that. So piloting or pre-testing is really important.

4.4 Look at the words that you wrote in the blanks in Ex 4.3 and answer the following questions.

a) Which words were stressed?

b) What kind of words were unstressed? How were these words pronounced? Was it difficult to hear them?

Sound advice: Some of the missing words in Ex 4.3 are unstressed and difficult to hear. Because they are function words, you do not usually need to understand them to follow the meaning. However, function words often show the relationships between ideas in the sentence, and so it can be important to understand them correctly.

Unit summary

In this unit you have discussed why it is important to take notes during a lecture and worked on your note-taking skills. You have also become more familiar with sentence stress and the difficulties of hearing unstressed words.

1   **Choose the correct option in each of these pieces of advice about effective note-taking.**

   a) During a lecture, you need to *write down everything you hear / be selective about what you write down*.

   b) You should try to *keep notes brief / write a lot to please your professor*.

   c) You need to make sure that *you / your professor* can understand the notes at a later date.

   d) You *have to write down key words related to the topic / don't need to write down key words because you will remember them anyway*.

   e) You should *always use complete sentences and words / sometimes use abbreviations to save time*.

   f) You should *make sure that the way points relate to one another is clear / note down points randomly because it is the quickest way to do it*.

2   **Complete each of these statements so that they are true for you. Delete any words you don't need.**

   a) I am happy that the notes I take usually _____ .

   b) When I look back at my notes later, I _____ .

   c) My notes are sometimes too _____ .

   d) I would like my notes to be (more) _____ .

3   **Look at this sentence and then answer the questions that follow.**

   It is important for you to learn how to take notes effectively during a lecture.

   a) Can you identify the three main stressed syllables in the sentence above?

   b) How quickly can you identify words that are weakened and more difficult to hear?

   c) Why is it useful to be aware of stressed words and syllables when you are listening to lectures?

   For web resources relevant to this unit, see:
   www.englishforacademicstudy.com/us/student/listening/links

Note-taking: Part 2

In this unit you will:
- learn how to use abbreviations and symbols to save time when note-taking;
- discuss the advantages and disadvantages of two ways of taking notes;
- practice note-taking from lectures.

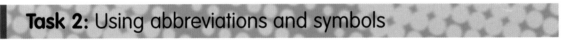

Task 1: Returning to your notes

It is important to make clear notes during lectures as you will need to understand them after the lecture or when you refer back to them later in the year. It is useful to look at the way others make notes, but in the end you will develop your own style.

Your instructor will show you some notes from a lecture extract that you listened to in Unit 4.

With a partner, see how you can expand the notes into complete sentences.

As you discuss, try to explain how the ideas are connected to one another.

> **Study tip**
>
> Remember that you will need your notes for future reference, so make sure they are clearly understandable.

Task 2: Using abbreviations and symbols

2.1 **What abbreviations and symbols were used in the notes in Task 1, and what do they mean?**

2.2 **Look at the examples of abbreviations that an economics student used. What do you think they stand for?**

> **Study tip**
>
> Your notes are generally for yourself, so the abbreviations you use will tend to be personal.

infl. _____	invest. _____	recess. _____
bus. _____	org. _____	min. _____

What abbreviations would you use if you were listening to lectures in your own field?

_____

_____

_____

2.3 What do you think the following symbols refer to?

Symbol	Meaning	Symbol	Meaning
↗	increase, rise, go up	≠	
↘		$	
→		?	
←		!	
⩾			

2.4 You are going to hear an extract from a lecture on language learning. The professor is referring to a source text (Littlewood, 1992) that provides an analysis of the purposes of education in general.

🎧 CD1 – 38 Listen and continue the following notes. Use symbols and abbreviations.

Extract 1

3 purposes of education (Littlewood, 1992)

2.5 You are going to hear an extract from a lecture on development economics. Here, the professor is describing changes in the world economy during the 1970s.

a) Before you listen, make sure you understand the meaning and pronunciation of the key vocabulary in the box.

b) 🎧 CD1 – 39 Listen and continue the following notes. Use symbols and abbreviations.

Extract 2

Vocabulary | inflation   anchored   devalue   float |

early 70s econ. boom ⇀ infl. in world econ.

Task 3: Organizing your notes

Different people organize their notes in different ways. Some students write linear notes, starting at the top of the page and working down, while other students prefer to use mind maps. The best solution may be to use different ways of taking notes for different types of lectures.

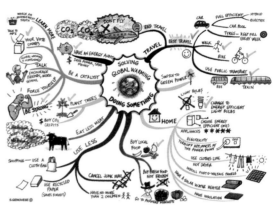

3.1 **Look at the following descriptions of different lectures. Do you think it would be better to use mind maps or linear notes for these lectures? Why? Discuss your ideas with a partner.**

a) This is a lecture on global warming.
The professor discusses the evidence that global warming is taking place, then looks at the causes, and finally looks at possible solutions and the difficulties of solving the problem.

b) This is a lecture on teleworking. The writer compares teleworking with normal ways of working, i.e., office-based working. He looks at the social, financial and environmental effects/benefits of both types of work.

c) This is a lecture on the history of the European Union from the 1950s to the present day.

d) This is the first lecture in a series of lectures on a course called *Global Problems*. In this lecture, the speaker gives an overview of some of the main problems facing the world today.

3.2 ⊙ CD1 – 40 **Listen to this extract from a lecture entitled *Health in the United States* and make notes. Work with a partner. One of you should take notes in a linear style, the other should make a mind map.**

a) Before you listen, make sure you know the words and phrases in the box. How would you abbreviate them?

individuals _____	life expectancy _____	statistics _____
heart disease _____	prescriptions _____	blood pressure _____
cholesterol _____	physical inactivity _____	National Center for Chronic Disease Prevention _____

b) Compare your notes with your partner. Which style of note-taking do you think was more appropriate for this lecture? Why?

3.3 **With your partner, discuss the advantages and disadvantages of linear notes and mind maps. Think about the following.**

● the process of writing the notes in a lecture;

● referring to the notes after the lecture.

3.4 **Compare your opinions with another pair.**

Task 4: Micro-skills: Word boundaries

4.1 ⊕ **CD1 – 41 Listen and complete the following sentences.**

a) The government has introduced ———————————— to encourage investment in this region.

b) For ———————————— , these organizations are often regarded as charities.

c) A number of reforms to the ———————————— have been proposed.

Did you find it difficult to understand the missing words in the sentences? If so, why?

4.2 The pronunciation of a word is affected by the word before or after it. When you are listening, it is sometimes difficult to hear when one word ends and another begins, because it may sound as if the words are linked together. In addition, sometimes sounds are inserted between the words, or sounds disappear or change. These make pronunciation easier for the speaker but may cause problems for the listener!

⊕ **CD1 – 42 Read the following explanation and listen to the examples.**

> **Linked words: Consonant + vowel**
>
> When a word ends in a consonant sound and the next word begins with a vowel sound, the words may seem to be linked, e.g.:
>
> add‿up
>
> What‿are these?
>
> the main‿objective
>
> **Inserted sounds: Vowel + vowel**
>
> When a word ends with a vowel sound and the next word begins with a vowel sound, a /w/ or /j/ sound is inserted, e.g.:
>
> do /w/ anything
>
> try /j/ out
>
> no /w/ idea of it
>
> **Disappearing/changing sounds: Consonant + consonant**
>
> When a word ends with a /d/ or /t/ sound and the next word begins with a consonant, the /d/ or /t/ sound often disappears, e.g.:
>
> next day
>
> rapid growth

4.3 🎧 **CD1 – 43** Listen to the following phrases. Mark the phrases with the symbols from Ex 4.2.

a) they invested in property

b) it's an open market

c) it's due on Friday morning

d) free admission on Sundays

e) it shows as a white mark

4.4 You are going to listen to an extract from a lecture on the theory of real options in investment.

Note: *Real options* are techniques that allow investments to be analyzed while taking flexibility and uncertainty into account.

🎧 **CD1 – 44** Listen and complete the text with two to five words in each blank. The missing expressions include examples of word boundaries that may cause you difficulties.

I'm going to go through the theory of real options, and then I'm going to show you how they can be used to _____, particularly on property assets. Real options are a term that was coined ten or 15 years ago, when people began to realize that _____ isn't the only thing you should look at in valuing assets, that a number of assets in companies have _____ option value. And so the option theory that you've been looking at can also be applied to _____ instead of just _____. And that, in raising money, companies particularly have _____ from an option pricing perspective than they first thought. The idea on real options is that management is not just a passive participant, that management can take _____ in making and revising decisions that can lead on from unexpected market developments, such as, for example, the _____ has gone up from $45 a barrel to _____ $80 a barrel over the last year. So if you were an oil producer this time last year you would be taking a very different view on the _____. So the increase in oil prices has uncovered a stream of options that make oil producers a lot more valuable and now you can bring oil fields _____ that were not necessarily economic. So this is the kind of idea that when we're looking at a project, we're not just looking _____, we're actually looking at a cash flow that can be subject to a lot of optionality in it.

Unit summary

In this unit you have seen how abbreviations and symbols can be used when taking notes, and you have discussed the advantages and disadvantages of two ways of taking notes. You have also looked at linking and word boundaries.

1   **Choose a, b, or c to complete each of these statements about note-taking.**

● Using abbreviations and symbols ...

   a)   saves time.
   b)   shows that you are intelligent.
   c)   stops other students from using your notes.

● If you use abbreviations and symbols ...

   a)   everyone must understand them.
   b)   your professor must understand them.
   c)   you must understand them.

2   **Delete the wrong options in this statement so that it is true for you.**

I *don't know how to use any / can use a few / use a number of* abbreviations and symbols when I take notes.

3   **Mark each of the different lecture types a–e below as follows.**

L—I think making linear notes is the better approach.
M—I think making a mind map is the better approach.

a)   The lecture discusses how successful one thing is compared with another and examines the reasons.

b)   The lecture runs through the history of an organization.

c)   The lecture is on an issue that affects everyone. It also gives examples of how the issue affects particular people in particular places.

d)   The lecture is about a successful person and outlines what he achieved in his life.

e)   The lecture states that a problem exists, examines its causes, and then proposes some solutions.

For web resources relevant to this unit, see:
www.englishforacademicstudy.com/us/student/listening/links

Listening

6 Introducing New Terminology

In this unit you will:
- listen to different professors introducing new terms or concepts;
- learn different techniques for introducing new concepts;
- practice recognizing unstressed function words that may be difficult to hear.

Task 1: Introducing new terminology

Professors usually introduce new terminology to their students during lectures. The terms they introduce often represent new or abstract concepts that can be difficult to grasp.

Here are some of the things professors do to help their students understand new terms or concepts.

- give definitions;
- provide a number of *extended* examples;
- explain how the term or concept works;
- contrast the new concept with a concept that is already familiar to the students.

In this unit you will listen to extracts from three lectures to see how professors deal with this issue.

Think about your own experience in lectures involving new terminology. How did the professor deal with it? What problems, if any, did you encounter? Discuss your experience with a partner.

Task 2: Lecture 1: Embedded words

In the following extract from a lecture on phonetics, the idea of *embedded words* is introduced by the professor. She gives an extended example of one embedded word to help explain the idea.

2.1 ⊕ CD2 – 1 **Listen to the extract and make notes on the extended example.**

Extended example:

2.2 **Check your notes with a partner. How would you define "embedded words"?**

2.3 **Think of at least one other example of an embedded word.**

Task 3: Lecture 2: Introducing terms and concepts (1)

In this lecture, the speaker looks at two different types of law within the European Union; directives and regulations. Before she explains the differences between the two types of law, she reminds the audience of some of the "key players" in the EU.

- the European Commission—a kind of civil service
- the Council of Ministers—a body that consists of the national ministers from each of the member states
- the European Parliament—which has 626 members elected from all the EU countries

3.1 **Before you listen, make sure that you understand the following words and phrases.**

minor technical matters	regulations come into force	opt out
visas and political asylum	become legally binding	pass a law

To explain the terms *regulations* and *directives* and the differences between them, the speaker talks about:

- who can issue them;
- what matters the two types of laws deal with;
- when they become legally binding.

3.2 ⊕ CD2 – 2 **Listen to the extract and complete the table.**

	Matters they deal with	Who issues them	When they become legally binding
regulations			
directives			

3.3 **Work with a partner. Using your notes from the table, take turns to explain fully what the terms *regulations* and *directives* mean.**

Task 4: Lecture 3: Introducing terms and concepts (2)

In this lecture, the speaker defines what he means by *dominance*. He does this partly by contrasting this new term with a term the students already know, *monopoly*.

4.1 **With a partner, discuss the meaning of the following words.**

dominance

monopoly

4.2 **Before you listen, make sure you understand the following words and phrases.**

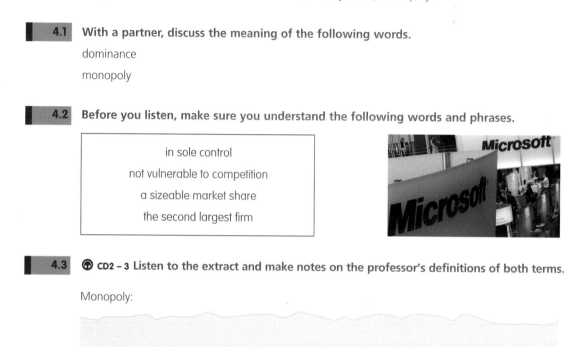

> in sole control
>
> not vulnerable to competition
>
> a sizeable market share
>
> the second largest firm

4.3 **CD2 – 3 Listen to the extract and make notes on the professor's definitions of both terms.**

Monopoly:

Dominance:

4.4 **Work with a partner. What examples of monopolies and dominant firms can you think of?**

Task 5: Micro-skills: Weak forms of function words

5.1 🎧 **CD2 – 4 Listen to the following pairs of sentences. What is the difference in the pronunciation of the *bold* words in each pair? What might explain this difference?**

a)
- What time **does** the train leave?
- I'm not sure why he's late. He **does** know about the meeting.

b)
- **Some** researchers have taken a different approach.
- We've just got time for **some** questions.

c)
- It was heated to 300°F **for** ten minutes.
- There are arguments **for** and against GM crop trials.

d)
- I'm not sure what you're getting **at**.
- There were **at** least five errors in the program.

e)
- Increasingly, small memory devices **can** store large amounts of data.
- Well, I **can** do it, but I don't want to.

f)
- Oh, are they going to interview **us** as well as the students?
- Can you tell **us** what you've found?

5.2 **Look back at the words in bold in Ex 5.1. Normally these words are unstressed. Why has the speaker chosen the stressed form in certain sentences?**

5.3 In the following extract from the lecture about market research, the professor is discussing the advantages and disadvantages of using multiple-choice questions.

🎧 **CD2 – 5 Listen and complete the extract with three to five words in each blank. In each case, at least one of the missing words is a function word.**

> Multiple-choice questions—easy. They reduce interviewer bias; very easy for people to … very easy and fast for people to answer; very _____ . But the argument goes that they are difficult to design. The thing about multiple-choice questions is that _____ people into certain answers. This is a good _____ . If you have a multiple-choice question and you pilot it, you may find that people are not, they don't put the issue that you're asking them into that particular _____ that you've imposed. So that's where _____ will help. Let me just show you an example of this.

Study tip

Many function words, e.g., conjunctions, articles, prepositions, and auxiliary verbs, are difficult to hear when they are unstressed.

Unit summary

In this unit you have listened to different professors introducing new terms or concepts and met different techniques for introducing new concepts. You have also practiced recognizing unstressed function words that may be difficult to hear.

1   **A professor has introduced the term *installment plan*. Match the techniques s/he could use to make the term clear (a–d) with the extracts (1–4).**

a)   give a definition ☐

b)   provide an example ☐

c)   explain how something works ☐

d)   contrast the new concept with a concept that is already familiar to the students ☐

1   The person buying the product pays for it over a period of time instead of paying for it all at once. They might make six payments of $200 or twelve payments of $100. Usually they will have to pay interest on top of that, which is why retailers are enthusiastic about the system.

2   Now, you all know what a loan is. You borrow money and pay it back at a later date. An installment plan is a sort of loan but …

3   An installment plan is one way that people can buy something— usually a fairly expensive product—in a way that they can afford. They make a number of payments instead of one large payment.

4   Say somebody wants a new sofa, but can not afford to pay one sum of $2,000. Well, one way around this is to …

2   **Check the technique a–d that you have found most helpful so far when trying to understand new concepts.**

3   **Look at this sentence and then answer the questions that follow.**

There are a number of different ways a professor can make new concepts easier for students to understand.

a)   How many function words can you identify in the sentence above that would probably be unstressed in normal speech?

b)   Write five more function words in your notebook.

c)   Why is it useful to be aware of unstressed function words when you are listening to lectures?

For web resources relevant to this unit, see:
www.englishforacademicstudy.com/us/student/listening/links

7 What Professors Do in Lectures

In this unit you will:
- think about how professors organize information in their lectures;
- discuss other ways of organizing information;
- practice recognizing ways of organizing information;
- practice note-taking;
- learn how word stress and pronunciation vary within word families.

Task 1: Introduction: Macro-structure of lectures

Writers use different structures to organize their writing. For example, they might use this structure.

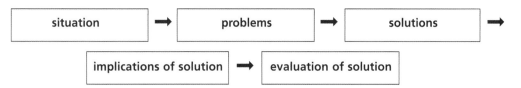

| situation | ➡ | problems | ➡ | solutions | ➡ |

| implications of solution | ➡ | evaluation of solution |

In a similar way, professors may also use different structures to organize their lectures. Here are some examples of what professors might do during a lecture.

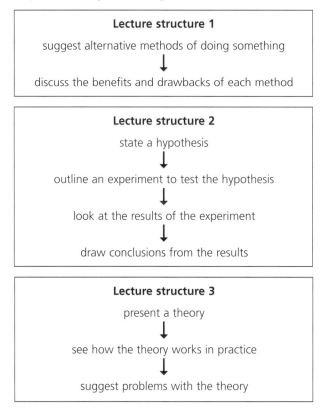

Lecture structure 1

suggest alternative methods of doing something
↓
discuss the benefits and drawbacks of each method

Lecture structure 2

state a hypothesis
↓
outline an experiment to test the hypothesis
↓
look at the results of the experiment
↓
draw conclusions from the results

Lecture structure 3

present a theory
↓
see how the theory works in practice
↓
suggest problems with the theory

Sound advice: Recognizing the structure of a lecture may help you understand the main ideas that the professor is trying to communicate. As you listen to a lecture, ask yourself:

- What is the professor doing at this point in the lecture?

- How does this part of the lecture relate to the other parts of the lecture?

These questions will help you get the "big picture"—i.e., the main ideas—of the professor's argument.

Think of lectures you have listened to. In groups, discuss the following questions.

a) Can you think of any lectures where the professors used these structures?

b) Can you think of any other ways professors organize their lectures?

Task 2: Lecture structure 1: Doing market research

In this lecture, the speaker is outlining different methods that market researchers use to get information from people. She also discusses the implications of each method.

2.1   **Before you listen, discuss the following questions in groups.**

a) Have you ever been asked to take part in a market research survey? What did you have to do? What kind of market research was it?

b) What do you think are the main ways of carrying out market research?

c) What are some advantages and disadvantages of each of the methods?

2.2   **CD2 – 6 The professor talks about four methods of market research in this lecture. Listen and complete the notes on the four methods.**

- computer-assisted telephone interviewing

-

-

-

2.3   **CD2 – 6 Listen again and make notes on any implications she mentions for any of the methods.**

Task 3: Lecture structure 2: Social learning

In this lecture, the speaker is looking at the hypothesis that animals learn from each other, for example, learning which foods to eat or avoid and which animals are their natural predators.

The professor discusses various experiments that have been used to test this hypothesis. She describes an experiment where a researcher took a group of "naive" monkeys that had been brought up in zoos. The monkeys had never encountered snakes and thus had no fear of them. These naive monkeys first observed a group of wild monkeys who were afraid of snakes. The researcher then tested the monkeys to see if their behavior had changed.

3.1   **Before you listen, discuss the following questions in groups.**

a) Do you think animals learn from each other? What do they learn and how?

b) What kind of experiments do you think researchers do to test social learning?

3.2 **CD2 – 7** Listen to Part 1 of the extract on how the experiments were carried out. Complete the notes.

Hypothesis:

It seems very plausible that monkeys in the wild learn to fear snakes from other monkeys who've already acquired the fear.

Experimental situation:

Observer monkeys

Timetable of experiment:

1 Pre-test

2 Post-test

3 Follow-up test

Label the two diagrams with these phrases: *neutral stimulus, glass box, food, model snake*. You will need to use some of the phrases more than once.

Procedure of experiments:

"Choice circus"

Wisconsin Test Apparatus

3.3 🔊 CD2 – 8 **Listen to Part 2 of the extract and make notes on the results and the conclusion the speaker draws from the results.**

Note: When giving the results, the speaker refers to a graph.

> **Results:**
>
> The models (the monkeys brought up in the wild):
>
> The observers (the monkeys brought up in zoos):
>
> **Conclusion:**

Task 4: Lecture structure 3: Contestable markets

In this lecture, the speaker is talking about *contestable markets*. He defines them as markets where entry and exit barriers do not exist or are low; in other words, it is easy or cheap for new suppliers to come into the market, and so existing suppliers have to worry about potential competition. The airline industry is commonly given as an example of such a market—especially now that there are many low-cost airlines.

The speaker begins by talking about the *theory* of perfect contestability and what the theory predicts. He then discusses the *problem* with this theory.

4.1 **Before you listen, make sure you understand the meaning of the following words and phrases.**

> marginal costs   undercut the price   in excess of   oligopolies
>
> inevitable delays   incur sunk costs   monopoly price

Do you think contestable markets are good for:

● the consumers;

● firms already in the market;

● firms that would like to come into the market?

4.2 🎧 CD2 – 9 **Listen to the extract and complete the notes below.**

Note: The speaker uses the term *incumbent firm* to refer to companies that are already in the market and the terms *an entry* and *the entrant* to refer to companies that would like to come into the market.

What the theory predicts:

Problems with the theory:

Task 5: Micro-skills: Word families (2)

Many nouns can be formed from verbs by adding a suffix. There may also be small changes in the spelling and pronunciation.

Examples:

Verb	Noun
describe /dɪsˈkraɪb/	description /dɪsˈkrɪpʃn/
prefer /prɪˈfɜːr/	preference /ˈprefrəns/
propose /prəˈpoʊz/	proposal /prəˈpoʊzl/

5.1 Change the verbs in the box into nouns and write them in the appropriate column in the table.

conclude   require   remove   fail   integrate   exist   dismiss
deduce   consume   acquire   proceed   amend   achieve
approve   compete   convert   resist   combine

~tion/~sion	~ance/~ence	~ment	~al	~ure

5.2 You will sometimes find that speakers use both verb and noun forms from the same word family in close proximity to one another. Here is an example.

> Although we had **decided** to focus our research on a limited range of fungi, it was a **decision** we were later forced to reassess.

🎧 CD2 – 10 Listen to the following short texts.

a) Make notes on the main points in the table below.

b) Listen again for a verb and noun from the same family in each extract.

Topic	Your notes	Verb and noun from same family
a) earthquakes		
b) hospital workers and radiation		
c) Japan's electronics industry		

table continued on page 49

Topic	Your notes	Verb and noun from same family
d) poverty		
e) behavior of particles		
f) road safety schemes		
g) male lions in Africa		
h) financial products		

5.3 You may find that, rather than using a verb and noun from the same family, in some cases you will hear synonyms.

🎧 CD2 – 11 **Listen to the following short texts and complete them with words or phrases that are synonyms.**

a) Many people are _____ that young people lack strong role models, and this _____ has prompted the police to question the conduct of professional athletes, whose actions may have a significant influence on young people.

b) The US decided to _____ the Moscow Olympics in 1980, in protest at the Soviet Union's invasion of Afghanistan. Four years later, the Soviet Union retaliated with its own _____ of the Los Angeles Olympics.

c) Many multinational companies prefer to _____ local enterprises. Such _____ have a number of advantages.

d) The public's _____ of the government's handling of the economy was critical. While the economy had in fact grown by two percent, people _____ the high unemployment rate and the government's inability to control strikes as indicators of poor performance.

Unit summary

In this unit you have looked at different ways that information in a lecture can be organized and practiced listening to lectures organized in different ways. You have also learned about word stress within word families.

1   **Think of three ways that the logical organization of a lecture helps you to understand and take notes.**

_____

_____

_____

2   **Put the stages of these two lectures into a logical order.**

Lecture 1

    a)   look at the results of the experiment

    b)   draw conclusions from the results

    c)   state a hypothesis

    d)   outline an experiment to test the hypothesis

1 ☐   2 ☐   3 ☐   4 ☐

Lecture 2

    a)   see how the theory works in practice

    b)   suggest problems with the theory

    c)   present a theory

1 ☐   2 ☐   3 ☐

3   **Work in pairs. Give your partner two pieces of advice about learning words from the same word family. Think about the form of the words and their pronunciation.**

_____

_____

For web resources relevant to this unit, see:
www.englishforacademicstudy.com/us/student/listening/links

8 Digressions

In this unit you will:
- look at examples of digressions in lectures;
- examine how professors sometimes mark the digressions;
- practice following the professor's main points;
- practice note-taking;
- learn a number of expressions commonly used in lectures.

Task 1: Reasons for digressions

In Unit 7 we looked at ways of organizing information. However, even where professors organize their information well and explicitly, they often move away from the main topic for a short time before returning to it. These are called *digressions*. There are a number of reasons why professors might digress during their lectures:

- to give a short definition of a new technical term;
- to give a reference to a book on the topic;
- to comment on the point they are making;
- to talk about the management of the lecture;
- to give general information about the course;
- to give a personal anecdote to illustrate a point.

When professors make digressions, these create problems for listeners. You have to:

- recognize that there is a digression;
- decide whether it is important to make a note or not;
- recognize when the professor has returned to the main point.

Think about your own experience in lectures. Do you enjoy lectures in which there are many digressions? Do you feel you learn more or less when the professor introduces digressions? Discuss your experiences with a partner.

Task 2: Identifying digressions

2.1 **Here is an example of a digression from the lecture on phonetics in Unit 6. The speaker is talking about the problem of embedded words.**

Read the text, including the highlighted digression. Why does the professor digress?

> The research that I've been involved in has been looking at factors responsible for our being able to cope successfully with this problem of embedded words, the fact that we're not constantly going off in the wrong direction being fooled by the sounds into hearing something that isn't there. Let's just try to think about what factors might be helping us not to go wrong. I've got three possible hypotheses here and again these are in the handout that I'll be giving you and you don't need to write these down, you'll get this text later on. OK, the question is then, how are we successful most of the time in deciding where word boundaries come?

2.2 Here is an example of a digression from the lecture on social learning in Unit 7. **CD2 – 12** Listen to the recording and read the extract. Then answer the following questions.

a) How many digressions does the professor make and why does she make them?

b) How does the professor mark the beginning and end of digressions?

> My first set of examples come from a—oh, but I'm going to talk about some fairly classic experiments in this lecture, but I would point out before I go on that there is a really excellent chapter on this subject in Shettleworth's book, which is referred to in the reference list for this lecture. Sara Shettleworth has a superb chapter on social learning. It's called "Learning from others." It's very up-to-date, very thoughtful, very comprehensive, and I'm just going to mention just a few of the examples that she mentions. But if you seriously want to think about this area, and it involves many complexities, her chapter is a very good place to go. Anyway, some of the best-known work on social learning, or putative social learning, in rats, in animals, are about food preferences. These are examples of learning the significance of stimuli, learning what foods are good to eat and what foods are bad to eat.

Task 3: Practice: Questionnaire design: Part 1

In this lecture, the speaker is talking about how to design questionnaires. In Part 1, he is talking about general design issues in preparing questionnaires.

3.1 **CD2 – 13** Listen to Part 1 and make notes on the main points of the lecture. **Do not make notes on the digression.**

With a partner, compare your notes.

3.2 **CD2 – 13** Listen again and pay attention to the digression. Answer the following questions.

a) What kind of information is the professor giving?

b) Would it be necessary to make a note of it?

3.3 CD2 – 13 **Listen again and read the transcript on page 83. How does the professor mark the beginning and end of the digression?**

Task 4: Practice: Questionnaire design: Part 2

In Part 2 of the lecture from Task 2, the professor is talking about what people need to do before they carry out market research using questionnaires.

4.1 CD2 – 14 **Listen to Part 2 and make notes on the main points. Do not make notes on the digressions.**

With a partner, compare your notes.

4.2 CD2 – 14 **Listen again and read the transcript on pages 83–84. How does the professor mark the beginning and end of the digression?**

Task 5: Practice: Integrated rural development

This is an extract from a lecture on the history of development economics. The speaker talks about a development program known as Integrated Rural Development (IRD).

In this extract, the professor:

- gives an explanation of IRD;
- gives an extended example to make his explanation clearer;
- comments on the IRD program;
- draws a conclusion.

During the lecture, the speaker also tells a personal anecdote.

5.1 The professor uses the following words and phrases in this extract. Before you listen, make sure that you understand them.

> fertilizer   combat   malaria
>
> an adult literacy campaign   synergy   filing cabinets

5.2 CD2 – 15 Listen and make notes on the main points. The four points in the introduction to this task will help you. Do *not* make notes on the digression.

With a partner, compare your notes.

Note: The speaker talks about Kenya to illustrate how the program worked. During the talk, he points to an outline map of Kenya and indicates parts of the country by saying, "there, there, and there."

5.3 CD2 – 15 Listen again and pay attention to the digression. Answer the following questions.

a) What kind of information is the professor giving?

b) Would it be necessary to make a note of it?

5.4 CD2 – 15 Listen again and read the transcript on pages 84–85. How does the professor mark the beginning and end of the digression?

Task 6: Micro-skills: Common expressions in lectures

In this activity, you will practice note-taking from short lecture extracts. In addition, you will focus on a number of expressions that commonly occur in lectures.

6.1 Extract 1 is from a professor on politics. The professor is discussing the issue of whether states are free to act as they please, or whether there are constraints on the way they act.

🎧 **CD2 – 16 Listen and complete the notes.**

> States can't _____ themselves from outside world. Growth of
> _____ states can't _____ what is going
> on around them. _____ has become more important, and
> states must respond. Strict appl. of _____ is being eroded.

6.2 🎧 **CD2 – 16 Listen again and complete the extract with one to four words in each blank.**

> I think that realism excludes the possibility—and it's a growing one—that states can simply isolate themselves from the outside world. The growth of television, the growth of mass communications, have meant that it's virtually impossible for states to ignore what is going on around them, and public opinion has become more important _____
> _____ within states, forcing states to do things that they might not otherwise do. So the strict application of power _____ maintaining the hierarchy, of ignoring the interests of others, is simply slowly being withered away.

With a partner, discuss what the expressions in the blanks mean.

6.3 Extract 2 is from a lecture on office design.

🎧 **CD2 – 17 Listen and complete the notes.**

> Scand. ideas impact on US office design.
> e.g., factors influencing unusual design of
> offices:

🎧 CD2 – 17 **Listen again and complete the extract with one to four words in each blank.**

… ten years later, therefore, we have the Scandinavian ideas impacting on American office design. Another illustration of that might be, you'll discover in _____ the lecture, that some of the factors that are driving the unusual, sometimes, configuration of office buildings, not always but sometimes, have _____ employment legislation; workers' councils, employers' rights, employees' rights.

With a partner, discuss what the expressions in the blanks mean.

6.5   Extract 3 is from the lecture on the history of development economics. The professor is discussing the impact of the 1982 debt crisis on financial assistance to developing countries.

🎧 CD2 – 18 **Listen and complete the notes.**

1982 – 1992: _____ did not lend money to dev.ing
world. Only lenders were:
      – other governments
      – _____
      – multilateral agencies, e.g., _____

6.6   🎧 CD2 – 18 **Listen again and complete the extract with one to four words in each blank.**

Nineteen eighty-two. None of the commercial banks gave any money to the developing world for _____ ten years after the '82 debt crisis. They got such a bad fright by the debt crisis they _____ ceased lending in the developing world. So the only people who were lending money to governments in the developing world from 1982 onwards were other governments, other aid agencies, and other multilateral agencies like the IMF and the World Bank.

With a partner, discuss what the expressions in the blanks mean.

Unit summary

In this unit you have discussed why professors sometimes mark digressions and looked at examples of the digressions they make. You have practiced following the professor's main points. You have also seen a number of expressions commonly used in lectures.

1 **Complete this summary with some of the words and phrases from the box.**

reference   main point   success   comment   recognize   explain

management   emphasize   anecdote   research

Even when professors organize their lectures well, they will sometimes digress from the main point. This might be to _____ further on the point they are making or in order to give a _____ to a book on the topic. They might want to give you some information about the course you are studying or say something about the _____ of the lecture they are giving at that moment. Professors will often tell students a personal _____ to illustrate a point they are making. When professors make digressions, it can create problems for listeners. To start with, you will need to _____ that there is a digression. Then you will need to decide whether the digression is important and whether you need to continue taking notes. Finally, you need to know when the professor has returned to the _____.

2 **Write one word or phrase that a professor might use to indicate that s/he is about to digress and another s/he might use to indicate that s/he is returning to the main point.**

_____

_____

3 **You want to give some advice to a classmate about words and phrases that professors commonly use in lectures. Write six examples in the blanks below.**

_____   _____

_____   _____

_____   _____

For web resources relevant to this unit, see:
www.englishforacademicstudy.com/us/student/listening/links

Abbreviation
A shortened form of a word or phrase, often used in notes or spoken English to save time, e.g., UN is an abbreviation of United Nations.

Academic word list
A list of some of the most wide-ranging and frequently used English words used in academic contexts. Students can use the AWL to find the most useful academic words that they need to know when they study at an English-speaking university.

Anecdote
A short account of an incident that is amusing or interesting.

Approach (to a subject)
A way of thinking about or dealing with something. An approach is less clearly defined or strict than a method.

Background noise
Sound that is not what you want to listen to and may prevent you from listening effectively to something else, e.g., if you are listening to someone talking to you in the street, you may find it difficult because of the background noise from the traffic.

Constraint
Something that limits what you are doing or want to do, e.g., there may be constraints of time, age, or language.

Content word
Words that carry meaning; usually nouns, verbs and sometimes adjectives and adverbs, e.g., the content words are highlighted in the following sentence: My <u>family</u> is <u>large</u>.

Critique
A review or commentary that criticizes something, e.g., a book, idea, or performance.

Digress/digression
To move away from the main point you are talking or writing about. Speakers sometimes digress when they are giving a lecture (often to tell a short story or personal anecdote) and then return to the central topic.

Embedded word
A word that forms part of a longer word, e.g., *cap* in *captain*. Embedded words may be confusing for students because they may have no connection with the topic under discussion.

Excerpt
A short extract or part of a recording or written text.

Function
The language used in particular situations or to convey certain ideas or needs. Introducing a topic, giving or asking for clarification, and criticizing are all different language functions.

Function word
A word that connects content words grammatically, but has little or no meaning by itself. Examples include articles, prepositions, and conjunctions, e.g., the function words are highlighted in the following sentence: <u>My</u> family <u>is</u> large.

Illustrate
To clarify using examples, comparisons or visual images.

Impact
An effect or strong impression.

Issue
A problem, topic or area for discussion or that needs to be worked on.

Linear notes
Notes that are arranged so that the ideas are grouped together in lines. The writer starts at the top of the page and works down to the bottom.

Listening strategy
Something that you can actively do to help your listening or improve your listening skills over a period of time. Typical listening strategies for a lecture include predicting what you are going to hear, picking out key words and signposts, and note-taking.

Macro-skills

Larger, more generalized skills that may consist of several different smaller skills (or sub-skills) that are used together. Listening is often referred to as a macro-skill itself, but it also involves the macro-skills of predicting and using background knowledge, recognizing how a lecture is structured, note-taking, etc.

Micro-skills

Skills that enable the student to piece together small pieces of information to build a bigger picture and make sense of something. Listening micro-skills include hearing which words are stressed or not stressed, recognizing where words begin and end in a stream of speech, etc.

Mind map

A diagram used to represent words, ideas, tasks, or other items linked to and arranged radially around a central key word or idea.

Preview

A short introduction or overview that gives an idea of what is going to happen in a lecture, film, or text.

Scope

The area covered by an activity or subject, e.g., a professor needs to limit the scope of a lecture.

Signal

Transmitting a message to others, usually through gesture. However, a signal can also be transmitted by specific words and phrases.

Signpost

Functional word(s) and/or phrase(s) that help to structure a spoken or written text and show the listener or reader where the speaker is going. For example, forward signposts may refer to what the speaker or writer is going to say next, e.g., *First I want to … then … finally*.

Stress

Word stress is the way in which one syllable in a word is given more force in a word or utterance. Stressed syllables or words are louder and longer than unstressed syllables. English places stress on key words or new information in a sentence, so students need to learn to recognize stressed words.

Stress pattern

The way that syllables are stressed or unstressed in a word, or words are stressed or unstressed in an utterance. The stress patterns of words may be different within a word family, e.g., *finance* but *financial*.

Syllable

A beat in a word. Each syllable has a vowel at its center and consonants "surround" the vowel. It is also possible to have a syllable with just a vowel. For example, the word *any* has two syllables (a-ny).

Terminology

Vocabulary (or terms) used in a particular field, topic or area of study. These may be technical words or terms to describe complex concepts that are specific to that topic.

Utterance

Something that one person says at a particular time. It could be a single word, a sentence, or a longer stretch of speech.

Weak form

Syllables and words that are not stressed in speech often have a different pronunciation or use weak forms in English. The full vowel sound is normally replaced with the schwa or /ə/ sound, e.g., "I can do it." (weak form) "Yes, I can!" (strong form).

Word boundary

The place where one word ends and another word begins. There are not always clear word boundaries in rapid connected speech because speakers normally join words together and change or drop sounds, particularly where words begin or end with a vowel sound, e.g., in the utterance: "I got up at eight o'clock" there may be no clear word boundaries.

Word family

A group of words that are closely related to each other because they share a common root or because they have related meanings, e.g., family, familiar, familiarize, familiarization.

Unit 1: Listening and Lectures

CD1 Track 1

Ex 2.2
Listen to Part 1 of a talk in which a professor describes some of the problems of listening.

Part 1

Many students find listening to and understanding spoken English particularly difficult, and I think there are a number of reasons for this.

First, there's the speed at which people talk. Obviously, when people are speaking quickly it's more difficult to understand them.

And then there's the issue of the topic that people are talking about. A topic you don't know much about is more difficult to understand than one you're familiar with. When you're listening to a familiar topic, you only need to concentrate on the new information, whereas if it's a new topic you often have to concentrate on just about everything.

There's also the problem of specialized vocabulary. There may be words you don't know. Now, if there are only a few words like this, people can generally follow the meaning, but if there are key words, or if there are a lot of unfamiliar words, then this can cause problems.

But there are two additional problems you may be faced with if English is not your first language.

When you're reading, you can see when one word ends and another one begins, because there's a space between them. But when you're listening, you can't. You often can't hear when one word ends and another begins, so you have to pick out the words you recognize and, from your understanding of the meaning, the context, and your knowledge of English grammar, fill in the blanks.

When students learn English, they're generally reading texts rather than listening to them, so they get used to the written forms of words rather than the spoken forms. But when they learn these words, they build up in their mind an expectation of their pronunciation. And when they actually hear these words in natural speech, they often fail to recognize the words, because they're pronounced in an unexpected way.

So, there are two problems; first, it's difficult for students to know when one word ends and another begins, and second, they often fail to recognize words that they know in the written form.

CD1 Track 2

Ex 2.3
Now listen to Part 2 of the talk, in which the professor illustrates the two problems she has introduced. The professor asks you to write down a phrase. Do this as you listen.

Part 2

So let's look at an example of this. I said earlier that students often fail to recognize words that they hear in natural speech. OK, so let's take the second part of that sentence, "words they hear in natural speech." Now I'd like you to take a pen and a piece of paper and write that part of the sentence down for me please. Just "words they hear in natural speech." That part. OK? So you're writing down "words they hear in natural speech." OK, so how many words are there in that phrase? Are there three? Four? Five? In fact there are six. "Words they hear in natural speech." Now when I said this at normal speed, you may have heard "hearinnatural" as one word, rather than three. And you may not have even recognized the word "natural," because you had an expectation that it might be pronounced /natural/ or as /naytural/, instead of /nætʃrəl/, which is how it is pronounced. You might have even heard the word *actual* or *national* instead of *natural*. But the point is, if you saw this phrase written down, you'd probably understand the meaning, but when you hear it, it's more difficult for you to understand.

CD1 Track 3

Ex 2.4
Listen to Part 3 of the talk. Complete this excerpt by writing two to six words in each blank.

Part 3

So what's the solution to these two problems? Well, first you need to get as much practice listening to natural speech as possible. Listen to extracts from lectures and try to develop your understanding of how words and phrases are really pronounced, not how you expect them to be pronounced. Secondly, you need to accept that when you listen you may misunderstand what is being said. So you need to be ready to change your mind about your understanding of the meaning, if what you hear doesn't make sense compared to what you understood before. And this means taking a flexible, open-minded approach to listening.

CD1 Track 4

Ex 3.2
Listen to Part 1 of the talk and make notes about the points.

Part 1

Good morning. I'm talking to you this morning because I'm interested in the differences between academic cultures in China and the US. Now, what I mean by "academic cultures" is simply how students study in the two countries; what are the different components of their courses, what instructors expect from them, and so on. And I'd like to present my ideas to you today and get some feedback from you. The thing I want to focus on particularly is lectures. I'm interested in the difference between lectures, both in terms of how the lectures are organized or presented and also in terms of how the lecture fits into the overall academic program.

Now, the first question I need to address is, "how do I know anything about lectures in China?" because I haven't studied there and in fact I haven't even been there. Well, I found out by interviewing Chinese students. What I did was conduct a kind of study called a tracking study. That means that you follow students over a period of time. What I did was to follow twelve Chinese students, all doing different courses, different masters degrees, and over their year of study I interviewed them three times individually. I interviewed them once in the fall, once in the spring, and then again in the summer. And the interviews lasted for about an hour, an hour and a quarter. I asked them a number of questions about studies in the US and about their studies in China. So my information comes from them, and so I have to say right from the beginning that I am talking here about information I got from twelve students, which is obviously a very small sample, and I don't know how representative what they said is of the Chinese education system as a whole. So we have to remember that limitation. I did choose different students from different parts of China, and I made sure that there was an equal number of men and women, and they were all studying different courses, so there was a range of backgrounds and experience. But there is that limitation. However, I felt that what I was hearing from the students was actually very similar. I mean, what they were saying individually was more or less the same. So I felt that maybe there is some basis for what they said, and maybe what they did say and maybe their experience was not untypical, in general, of students in China.

CD1 Track 5

Ex 3.4
In Part 2 of the talk, the professor first talks about some of the characteristics of lectures in China and then compares these with lectures in the US. Listen and make notes on the main points he makes.

Part 2

OK, so what did I find out? I think the first thing to say is that my impression is that in China the lecture delivers a lot of the content of the course, or the professor delivers a lot of the content of the course. And this seems to be especially true at undergraduate level. And just to reinforce this, the students I talked to were graduate students. In other words, they'd done undergraduate studies in China. I'm not sure about graduate studies in China. But what they said about undergraduate courses was that a lot of the course content came through the lectures. In other words, the students go to the lectures, they make notes in the lectures, and at the end of the term, or at the end of the year, if they have a test or exam, in many cases they simply give back to the professor what the professor gave to them during the lectures. And that seems to be sufficient to pass the exam and pass the course. So, the lecture is the important vehicle of the course content; it carries the course content.

Now, the second point they made about lectures was that in China they don't seem to be very interactive, in the sense that students sit, they listen, they take lots and lots of notes. But they don't often ask questions during the lecture or at the end of the lecture, and they don't have much discussion, either during or at the end of the lecture, and that is not expected of them. So they really, in China, lectures don't seem to be very interactive.

Another point that students made to me, which I thought was interesting, was that the main points, the important points of a lecture, are often explicitly marked by the professor. The professor might say, "OK, this point is very important, make a note of this" and might even write things on the blackboard, which the students would copy down verbatim. In other words, they would copy down exactly what he was writing. So this was interesting, it seems that the students don't have to decide for themselves what is important, what is less important. The professor tells them. Now obviously that's a very general and very rough caricature of what students told me about Chinese lectures. But how does that compare with the situation in the US?

Well, here, I think it's fair to say that the course content is not only delivered through the lectures. If you take a course in an American university and if you only give back to the professor in exams, or tests, or assignments or essays, if you only give back what he or she says during the lecture, then I don't think you are going to pass the exam. I think what professors are doing in the US is something different. I think either they are giving an overview of the main ideas connected with the subject, or they are giving some general background to the subject, and then it's the student's responsibility to go away, and to do lots of reading, and to really fill in the details, and to fully understand the theories, the ideas the professor is talking about.

And that really brings me to the point of reading. Because what I understood from my Chinese students was that in China, certainly at undergraduate level, they had one course book for each course, and just to emphasize that, they seemed to have one textbook. And there was a very close correspondence between what the professor was saying and what was in the textbook. In other words, if the students wanted to, they could go away at the end of the lecture and read the textbook, and it would essentially say what the professor himself had said, so there was that kind of reinforcement. Here, it is very different. There's not normally one textbook for one course. You can't just go away and read one book, and find the entire content of the lectures there. You will have to read a lot of books and a lot of articles to fill in what the professor has given you. So in this country, reading, and reading really widely, is an essential part of what students do after lectures. In China it seems that there is a lot less reading, and the reading is mainly concentrated on this one textbook.

That's one thing about the US. The other thing about the US, lectures here, is that professors here do expect students to interact, to ask questions, to raise points of view, to make comments, to enter into discussion. Now obviously how much discussion there is, how much interaction there is, depends very much on how many students there are in the lecture. In this university, for example, in some cases, we may have 20 students in a lecture and in other cases we may have 200 students in a lecture and obviously there's less discussion if there are more students. There's less time for questions. But interactiveness in general is very important at universities here in this country.

Well, those are just some of my impressions of the differences between lectures in China and the USA, but I would really be very interested now in hearing your opinions. Whether you think what I've talked about is true from your experience or not.

Unit 2: Introductions to Lectures

CD1 Track 6

Ex 1.4
Listen to the introduction. Then answer the questions.

Migration

There's been a lot of talk in the newspapers and on television since 9/11 about immigration to the United States from countries in the Arab world like Syria and Jordan. This discussion is centered on questions like whether this has an effect on the security of the US, as well as questions about the impact of cultural differences between the two regions, etc. However, that's not the type of migration that I want to look at today. What I want to look at is internal migration, i.e., the movement of people from country to city, and vice versa, and from one city to another.

CD1 Track 7

Ex 3.2
Listen to the introduction to the lecture *Britain and the European Monetary Union*. Which aspects from the checklist in Task 2 does the professor use?

Britain and the European Monetary Union

OK, good morning. Can you all hear me? Good. OK, let's get started. Well, today I'm going to be talking to you about Britain and EMU, the European Monetary Union. As you know, the United States is already a monetary union significantly larger than Western Europe, and it was this model that was used in Europe. As you may know, there are now 13 countries in the EMU, or Eurozone as it's popularly known; the last country to join being Slovenia in 2007. You also probably know that Britain has not joined the Eurozone. Incidentally, the UK isn't alone in this, as other EU countries have also opted out, for example, Denmark. I'll come back to the reasons the UK hasn't yet joined later in the lecture.

Now, I have already talked in previous lectures about the early history of the European Union, or the European Economic Community, as it was originally known, and I also talked about the reasons Britain was reluctant to join the EEC, and why some other members of the EEC, France in particular, were not convinced that Britain should join either. One of the main reasons for this was, I suggested, that Britain felt it had a special relationship with the United States and with its former colonies in the Commonwealth and didn't want to endanger this relationship by joining. And after Britain's participation in the wars with Iraq, you might conclude that the British still believe they have a special relationship with the US—even if we in the US may not always see this in the same way.

However, leaving all that aside, today I want to talk about three things. Firstly, I am going to talk about the process of how the euro was introduced, and then I'm going to talk about the economic and political tests that a new country has to pass in order to join the euro. However, as the title of my lecture suggests, I'm going to spend most of the time today talking about why Britain has not adopted the euro, and then about whether I think Britain might join the Eurozone in the future and in what circumstances.

CD1 Track 8

Ex 3.4
Listen to the introduction to the lecture *Globalization*. Which aspects from the checklist in Task 2 does the professor use?

Globalization

Globalization is a term that you hear everywhere these days, whether people are talking about food—McDonald's and other fast-food companies in particular—or about the economy, with more and more multinational companies all over the world, or about information, with the Internet and the spread of the English language making the same information available at the same time to people all over the world.

Arguably, globalization also includes national cultures, with some authorities suggesting, as I myself do in my latest book, that national cultures as we knew them no longer exist. In any case, globalization is often said to be the single most profound and wide-ranging change in human history. Ever. Well, that is something you can discuss later, you may have your own opinions on whether this is true or not. But it does go without saying that it is something that affects everybody's life; it affects people as diverse as farmers in the Third World, stockbrokers in New York and London; or global tycoons in multimillion-dollar empire industries. So, obviously, this is something in which a political scientist, or, for that matter, an historian, or sociologist, or geographer, or a whole range of other disciplines, might well be interested.

What I'm going to try to do today is give you some understanding of the history of globalization, what globalization means to people on a local level, and what its implications could be for the whole world.

So I'm going to be talking on a global scale—which is appropriate for this topic—and I'm also going to be covering some fairly long periods of time.

CD1 Track 9

Ex 3.6
Listen to the introduction to the lecture *District Courts*. Which aspects from the checklist in Task 2 does the professor use?

District Courts

Good morning, everybody. In spite of what John just said, I'm not going to spend a lot of time talking about the family work. That is a specialist area of the District Court. As John says, it deals with one aspect of legal disputes involving the state and children. So, for example, in the case of family breakup, it would involve making parental contact orders where the parents can't agree on how much contact time each parent should have with the child, after divorce for example. It also deals with parental responsibility. That means fathers who are refusing to pay for the maintenance of their children. Then finally it deals with any kind of case involving the state and the child. Notably when the state wishes to take the child from the care of the parents and put it in the care of somebody else or in the care of the government, and also when the child is to be adopted by another family. But that's another specialist area. What we're mainly concerned with today is criminal offenses, and that's what I'm going to spend most of my time talking about this morning.

So this is a court—the District Court deals with all offenses, including criminal offenses. But we're not here to talk about things like, for example, disputes between neighbors. For example, if you have an argument with your neighbor about the noise that's being made, or the height of his hedge that's preventing the light from getting into your garden—all these kinds of things are dealt with in the District Court, but here we're dealing with criminal cases so it's crimes against the state as defined by the legal code. So I just want to make that clear from the beginning.

So within that criminal justice system, first of all we're dealing with State law here. There's a different system that operates at the Federal level, although they have the same system of Trial Courts, Intermediate Appeal Courts and a Supreme Court—so we're talking about the district level only. We're not dealing with offenses related to Federal criminal law such as evading federal income tax, but those that are dealt with at State level, and that is the District Court.

CD1 Track 10

Ex 4.1
Listen and complete the sentence from the introduction to *Britain and the European Monetary Union*.

However, as the title of my lecture suggests, I'm going to spend most of the time today talking about why Britain has not adopted the euro, and then about whether I think Britain might join the Eurozone in the future and in what circumstances.

CD1 Track 11

Ex 4.2
Listen and complete the following sentences from the introduction to *District Courts*. Write one word in each blank.

So, for example, in the case of family breakup, it would involve making parental contact orders where the parents can't agree on how much contact time each parent should have with the child.

What we're mainly concerned with today is criminal offenses, and that's what I'm going to spend most of my time talking about this morning.

CD1 Track 12

Ex 4.4
Listen to a recording about security and computers. Complete the text with one word in each blank. Use words from Ex 4.3.

Security is an important aspect of using a computer that many people don't pay much attention to. If you buy a laptop or personal computer, you'll probably want to connect to the Internet. If so, it's important that you install security software that'll protect it from attack by viruses or spyware. Now there is a wide range of products available on the market that are relatively cheap and that provide a variety of different features. For example, in addition to checking their computer for viruses, parents can use the software to control which websites their children can access. You shouldn't assume, however, that you are 100 percent safe if you're using such security software. You should make sure that you have backup copies of your work, and you should be very careful about keeping important information, such as bank account details, on your computer.

CD1 Track 13

Ex 4.5
Listen to a recording about competition between large supermarket chains and small local shops in the UK. Complete the text with one word in each blank. All the words begin with *con~*, *pro~* or *a~*.

As in the United States, supermarket chains in the UK are always looking for new opportunities. Because of planning restrictions, the large UK chains are currently looking to expand their businesses and increase profits by opening smaller "convenience stores." Organizations representing small, independent shops protest that they now face unfair competition from the large chains. And they accuse the large chains of a number of practices that make it difficult for them to compete. First, it's alleged that below-cost pricing is used by large supermarkets to force smaller, local shops out of business. Second, the large chains often buy up land that is not immediately used, and this prevents smaller local businesses from entering the market.

There is also some concern that the large chains are treating UK suppliers unfairly. Farmers claim that they are being paid less for their products, and are reluctant to complain for fear of losing key contracts.

However, supermarkets argue that the consumer is the best regulator of the market.

CD1 Track 14

Ex 4.7
Listen to a recording about the effect of global warming on numbers of polar bears. Complete the text with one word in each blank. Use words from Ex 4.6.

Wildlife experts predict that numbers of polar bears will decline by at least 50 percent over the next 50 years because of global warming. Polar bears rely on sea ice to catch seals for food, and it's emerged that ice floes in the Arctic are disappearing at an alarming rate. Scientists report that the animals are already beginning to suffer the effects of climate change in some parts of Canada, and if there is any further delay in tackling this problem, polar bears may be extinct by the end of the century.

Ex 4.8

Listen to a recording about monitoring water levels in rivers. Complete the text with one word in each blank. All the words begin with *de~*, *re~* or *e~*.

Scientists are now able to monitor river levels using information from satellites by using a computer program devised by researchers at De Montfort University in Leicester in the UK. Satellites have been able to measure the height of the sea by timing how long it takes to receive a beam bounced back off waves. But until now, interference from objects on the banks of rivers has made it impossible to measure river levels. However, the new program, which is based on data collected over the last decade, is specially designed to filter out this interference. This new technology will be particularly useful in monitoring river levels in remote areas. It will, for example, enable scientists to examine river level patterns over the entire Amazon river basin, contributing towards our understanding of climate change.

Unit 3: Identifying Key Ideas in Lectures

CD1 Track 16

Ex 2.2

Listen to Part 1 of the lecture, which is in three sections. Identify the three sections and put them in the correct order.

Franchising

Part 1

Section 1

The form of business development I'm going to look at now is franchising. The term "franchising" covers a wide range of business arrangements, but today I'm going to focus on "business format franchising."

If you own a small or medium-sized enterprise, you may reach a stage in its development at which, in order to develop further, you need large amounts of capital, or you need to reorganize your business, or to bring into the management team new skills. Let's say you own four or five hairdressing salons in your city that are very profitable. You want to expand the business, but recognize first that a lot more money will need to be invested, and secondly that you will not be able to exert the same amount of personal control over the day-to-day running of the business that you have been used to. This stage in the growth of the business may present the entrepreneur with risks that he or she is unwilling to run. However, one way of minimizing such risks, while at the same time continuing to develop and profit from a successful brand, is by franchising your business.

Section 2

So, what is franchising? Well, here is a definition from an online business glossary. And it says, "A form of business organization in which a firm that already has a successful product or service (the franchisor) enters into a continuing contractual relationship with other businesses (franchisees) operating under the franchisor's trade name and usually with the franchisor's guidance, in exchange for a fee." This package would include things like training, consultancy arrangements, possibly supplies, marketing on a national scale, etc.

Section 3

So, for example, if you own a group of successful fast-food restaurants trading under the same name, you may decide to run your business as a franchise. You would allow other businesspeople to open their own branches of the fast-food chain, using your trademark, and in fact you would probably supply a lot of the signage and materials necessary to maintain a uniform brand. In return, the franchisee pays you, the franchisor, an initial fee, that is to say a fee paid at the beginning of the business arrangement, and also an ongoing management service fee. This management service fee is related to the volume of business the franchisee is doing, so it might be calculated as a percentage of turnover, or as a mark-up on supplies provided by the franchisor. So there are two kinds of the fee, the one-time initial fee to set up the franchise, and the ongoing management service fee.

CD1 Track 17

Ex 2.3
Listen to Part 1 Section 1 again and answer the questions.

Section 1

The form of business development I'm going to look at now is franchising. The term "franchising" covers a wide range of business arrangements, but today I'm going to focus on "business format franchising."

If you own a small or medium-sized enterprise, you may reach a stage in its development at which, in order to develop further, you need large amounts of capital, or you need to reorganize your business, or to bring into the management team new skills. Let's say you own four or five hairdressing salons in your city that are very profitable. You want to expand the business, but recognize first that a lot more money will need to be invested, and secondly that you will not be able to exert the same amount of personal control over the day-to-day running of the business that you have been used to. This stage in the growth of the business may present the entrepreneur with risks that he or she is unwilling to run. However, one way of minimizing such risks, while at the same time continuing to develop and profit from a successful brand, is by franchising your business.

CD1 Track 18

Ex 2.4
Listen to Part 1 Section 2 again. In pairs, discuss what the terms mean in the context of the lecture.

Section 2

So, what is franchising? Well, here is a definition from an online business glossary. And it says, "A form of business organization in which a firm that already has a successful product or service (the franchisor) enters into a continuing contractual relationship with other businesses (franchisees) operating under the franchisor's trade name and usually with the franchisor's guidance, in exchange for a fee." This package would include things like training, consultancy arrangements, possibly supplies, marketing on a national scale, etc.

CD1 Track 19

Ex 2.5
Listen to Part 1 Section 3 again.

Section 3

So, for example, if you own a group of successful fast-food restaurants trading under the same name, you may decide to run your business as a franchise. You would allow other businesspeople to open their own branches of the fast-food chain, using your trademark, and in fact you would probably supply a lot of the signage and materials necessary to maintain a uniform brand. In return, the franchisee pays you, the franchisor, an initial fee, that is to say a fee paid at the beginning of the business arrangement, and also an ongoing management service fee. This management service fee is related to the volume of business the franchisee is doing, so it might be calculated as a percentage of turnover, or as a mark-up on supplies provided by the franchisor. So there are two kinds of the fee, the one-time initial fee to set up the franchise, and the ongoing management service fee.

Ex 3.2
Listen to Part 2 of the lecture.

Part 2

Section 1

There are a number of issues you need to consider when deciding whether or not to franchise your business. First, there needs to be a relatively stable, long-term market for the product or service you are franchising. This is partially because substantial investment in time and money is required to set up and develop a franchise operation, and partly because you need an established market with potential for long-term growth to attract franchisees. So, something like a chain of hairdressing salons might offer potential for a franchise, because there will always be a demand for women to have their hair cut and styled. On the other hand, a franchise to promote and sell a new kind of children's toy might be less successful because toys tend to have a short market lifespan.

Section 2

In addition—and this is fairly obvious—you will need a fairly wide margin between cost and income. Remember that the gross margin needs to provide a return on the investment to both the franchisor and the franchisee. So you will need to keep costs low and prices as high as the market will bear. One advantage of a franchise operation is that supplies can be bought in bulk across the whole franchise, which will help to keep costs down. But you can see that franchising would be unsuitable in a market where the margin between cost and income is very narrow.

Section 3

The franchisor will need to provide support and training to the franchisee because, in addition to the brand, what you are selling is a way of doing business that has proved successful. You will need to produce an operating manual that describes in detail all the different systems and procedures involved in the business, and the performance and quality standards, but you will also have to provide some kind of training for the franchisee and possibly his employees, certainly in setting up the operation and possibly on a regular, ongoing basis. The important point here is that for a franchise to be successful, it should be possible for the franchisee to develop the skills required to operate the business fairly quickly. So, although some initial training may be required, the franchisee should be able to operate the business efficiently and successfully within a few months of start-up. In some types of franchise the skills required may be acquired quickly, in others the franchisee may have already developed most of the necessary skills in previous employment. So, for example, someone operating a franchise in the restaurant industry is likely to have experience either as an employee in a restaurant, or in a similar field.

Ex 3.4
Listen to Part 2 Sections 1 and 2 again and answer the following questions.

Section 1

There are a number of issues you need to consider when deciding whether or not to franchise your business. First, there needs to be a relatively stable, long-term market for the product or service you are franchising. This is partially because substantial investment in time and money is required to set up and develop a franchise operation, and partly because you need an established market with potential for long-term growth to attract franchisees. So, something like a chain of hairdressing salons might offer potential for a franchise because there will always be a demand for women to have their hair cut and styled. On the other hand, a franchise to promote and sell a new kind of children's toy might be less successful because toys tend to have a short market lifespan.

CD1 Track 22

Section 2

In addition—and this is fairly obvious—you will need a fairly wide margin between cost and income. Remember that the gross margin needs to provide a return on the investment to both the franchisor and the franchisee. So you will need to keep costs low and prices as high as the market will bear. One advantage of a franchise operation is that supplies can be bought in bulk across the whole franchise, which will help to keep costs down. But you can see that franchising would be unsuitable in a market where the margin between cost and income is very narrow.

CD1 Track 23

Ex 3.5
Listen to Part 2 Section 3 again, where the professor talks about: training and support, the operating manual, and developing skills quickly.

Section 3

The franchisor will need to provide support and training to the franchisee because, in addition to the brand, what you are selling is a way of doing business that has proved successful. You will need to produce an operating manual that describes in detail all the different systems and procedures involved in the business, and the performance and quality standards, but you will also have to provide some kind of training for the franchisee and possibly his employees, certainly in setting up the operation and possibly on a regular, ongoing basis. The important point here is that for a franchise to be successful, it should be possible for the franchisee to develop the skills required to operate the business fairly quickly. So, although some initial training may be required, the franchisee should be able to operate the business efficiently and successfully within a few months of start-up. In some types of franchise the skills required may be acquired quickly, in others the franchisee may have already developed most of the necessary skills in previous employment. So, for example, someone operating a franchise in the restaurant industry is likely to have experience either as an employee in a restaurant, or in a similar field.

CD1 Track 24

Ex 4.1
Listen to Part 3 of the lecture. Make notes on the key points in your notebook. Then compare your notes with a partner. Have you identified the same key points?

Part 3

Section 1

One further issue you may need to consider is whether the business is transferable to another geographical area. If you have developed your business serving one particular part of the country and you want to set up a franchise network covering a much larger area, the whole country for example, another thing you will have to consider is whether there is a similar market for your product or service in different regions. It may be, for example, that competition in other parts of the country may be so strong that it is difficult for franchisees to survive, or that for localized socioeconomic or cultural reasons the business may not be as profitable.

Section 2

Finally, when you are setting up a franchise network, you will need to bear in mind that you will be losing direct control of the way your brand is perceived by the customer, so this brings me to my last point, which is to emphasize the importance of protecting your brand. I am sure you are all aware that it often takes a long time to establish a distinctive brand with a valuable reputation, but that this reputation can be damaged comparatively quickly if, for example, quality standards are not consistently applied. The detailed operating manual that I referred to earlier will play a role in maintaining the brand but, just as important, you need to take care selecting franchisees and monitoring their operations. In addition to checking that franchisees have the relevant skills and experience to run a successful business, you also need to ensure that they share the same business values as you, that they accept the importance of maintaining the brand and that they are clear about what they can or can't change about the way the business is run—so people who are very individualistic will probably not make good franchisees.

Section 3

The written agreement between the franchisor and the franchisee should specify very clearly what performance and quality standards are expected, and much of the initial training will be ensuring that staff have the skills to achieve these standards. However, regular visits to franchise units are essential in ensuring that the standards are being applied consistently and uniformly, and ongoing training may be necessary to deal with issues that are uncovered in these visits. Protecting the brand is ultimately in the interests of both the franchisor and the franchisee, because for the franchisee one of the main advantages in running a franchise is that they are buying into and helping to consolidate an established brand.

CD1 Track 25

Ex 4.2
Listen to Part 3 Section 1 again and complete the excerpt with one to three words in each blank.

Section 1

One further issue you may need to consider is whether the business is transferable to another geographical area. If you have developed your business serving one particular part of the country and you want to set up a franchise network covering a much larger area, the whole country for example, another thing you will have to consider is whether there is a similar market for your product or service in different regions. It may be, for example, that competition in other parts of the country may be so strong that it is difficult for franchisees to survive, or that for localized socioeconomic or cultural reasons the business may not be as profitable.

CD1 Track 26

Ex 4.3
Listen to Part 3 Sections 2 and 3 again. Make notes on the different ways in which brands can be protected.

Section 2

Finally, when you are setting up a franchise network, you will need to bear in mind that you will be losing direct control of the way your brand is perceived by the customer, so this brings me to my last point, which is to emphasize the importance of protecting your brand. I am sure you are all aware that it often takes a long time to establish a distinctive brand with a valuable reputation, but that this reputation can be damaged comparatively quickly if, for example, quality standards are not consistently applied. The detailed operating manual that I referred to earlier will play a role in maintaining the brand but, just as important, you need to take care selecting franchisees and monitoring their operations. In addition to checking that franchisees have the relevant skills and experience to run a successful business, you also need to ensure that they share the same business values as you, that they accept the importance of maintaining the brand and that they are clear about what they can or can't change about the way the business is run—so people who are very individualistic will probably not make good franchisees.

CD1 Track 27

Section 3

The written agreement between the franchisor and the franchisee should specify very clearly what performance and quality standards are expected, and much of the initial training will be ensuring that staff have the skills to achieve these standards. However, regular visits to franchise units are essential in ensuring that the standards are being applied consistently and uniformly, and ongoing training may be necessary to deal with issues that are uncovered in these visits. Protecting the brand is ultimately in the interests of both the franchisor and the franchisee, because for the franchisee one of the main advantages in running a franchise is that they are buying into and helping to consolidate an established brand.

CD1 Track 28

Ex 5.3

You can also modify the meaning of a word by adding a prefix, for example, *interpret/misinterpret, assess/reassess, appear/disappear*. Listen to the following sentences and write in the missing prefix to each word. How do the prefixes change the meaning of the original words?

a) All unions were declared illegal by the government.

b) This is one example of a mismatch between the individual's goals and those of the organization.

c) They found no significant correlation between class size and levels of achievement.

d) Real estate transactions rose by 30 percent last month.

e) Prices are determined through the interaction of supply and demand.

f) These animals exhibited abnormal behavior compared to the control group.

CD1 Track 29

Ex 5.4

Listen to the following sentences and complete them with two to four words in each blank. Some of the words include prefixes.

a) We had to get the photos enlarged, because the detail was not very clear on the original ones.

b) Many doctors work long, irregular hours, which puts them under a lot of stress.

c) Crime prevention is an important aspect of the police's work, but it is often difficult to assess its effectiveness.

d) Doctors have noticed an increase in eating disorders, such as bulimia and anorexia, not just among young women but, surprisingly, among young men.

e) These plants should be grown in partial shade, rather than in direct sunlight.

f) Researchers have found that inexperienced drivers are much more likely to be involved in traffic accidents.

CD1 Track 30

Ex 5.5

Listen to the following groups of sentences. Complete the sentences with two to four words in each blank. One of the words in each blank is a form of the word in bold.

a) Children need a **secure** environment in which to grow up.

Many immigrants are only able to find low-paid, insecure jobs.

The money was invested in securities and property.

b) Achievement levels **vary** considerably from school to school in the city.

Some economists believe that interest rates can be predicted by examining key economic variables.

In the UK's Eden Project, they have managed to create a wide variety of habitats.

There is significant variation in access to health care in different parts of the country.

c) How are we going to **solve** this problem?

You need to dissolve the pesticide in water before applying it to the crop.

There appears to be insoluble conflict between the two countries, despite years of peace negotiations.

d) A mass spectrometer was used to **analyze** the gases.

Further analysis of the data is needed to confirm these initial findings.

The course is designed to help students to develop their analytical skills.

e) The results **indicate** that the virus mutates more rapidly than was first believed.

All the main economic indicators suggest that the economy is recovering.

The strike was indicative of the level of the workers' frustration.

f) Chomsky was a fierce **critic** of Bush Senior's foreign policy.

There was some criticism of the way the election had been administered.

The negotiations were critical to establishment of peace in the area.

Unit 4: Note-taking: Part 1

CD1 Track 31

Ex 2.2
Listen to the recording and read the text at the same time.

America's transport problems

Part 1

So America's roads, and especially those in urban areas, are overcrowded. There are too many cars on the roads, and at particular times of the day and at particular places, traffic is either very slow or at a standstill. Now this has had a number of effects. First there is the economic effect, all the time wasted in traffic jams, which means a loss of productivity. Then there's the environmental effect. Cars produce a lot of pollution, which damages the local environment, but it also contributes to global warming. And there's also the effect on people's health. In addition to the poor air quality and the damage this causes to people's lungs, the stress of being stuck in traffic each day leads to a higher risk of heart disease.

CD1 Track 32

Ex 2.6
Listen to Parts 2–4 of the lecture and continue the notes. Before you listen, make sure you understand the meaning and pronunciation of the words in the boxes.

Part 2

So how do we deal with this problem? It is widely accepted among researchers and policy makers that there isn't just one simple solution. For example, it's generally agreed that simply building more roads is not the solution, as research shows that this just leads to an increase in traffic and, in the long term, it worsens the problems that I've just described. So what is needed is a whole range of measures aimed at improving the transport system. This is referred to in the UK as "integrated transport policy," and it is interesting to look at what they are doing over there, where there is much more overcrowding.

Part 3

In 1997 the British government carried out a major public consultation on the UK's integrated transport policy. One of the main issues addressed was how we can encourage car drivers to use public transport. The first point is that just making improvements to the public transport system will not be enough to get drivers to use buses or trains. We can provide more buses and trains so that these are less crowded, and we can make them cleaner, safer environments to travel in, and all this will need more investment of course, but even if we do all this, drivers will still prefer to use their cars.

Part 4

So, as I said, it is recognized that we need a package of measures to reduce the number of vehicles on the road. Here are some examples.

As you know, car-sharing is already well established in the US, with many Internet sites offering support. In Britain, the government itself is trying to encourage car-sharing, so, in some experimental projects on crowded roads, lanes have been designated for use only by cars with more than one occupant; CCTV cameras are used to police the trials. The thinking is that if people believe they can get to work more quickly by driving in this faster lane, they are more likely to share cars.

In London, congestion charging has been successful; cars are charged to enter a central zone and again CCTV cameras linked to a computer system are used to ensure compliance. The effect has been that there are fewer cars in what used to be the busiest part of London, but in addition, the income from congestion charging is then invested in London's public transport system. Here in the US, it is generally agreed that it would be difficult to get public support for such proposals, however.

Well, these are just two examples of fairly small-scale, localized solutions to the problem, but to sum up the point I made earlier, a whole range of measures attacking the problem from different angles is more likely to be successful than one "big idea."

CD1 Track 33

Ex 3.1
Listen to Part 1 of an extract from a lecture on the history of development economics. The professor is discussing the reasons for rapid economic growth in East Asia in the 1980s.

The East-Asian economic miracle

Part 1

And a lot of time was spent in the nineteen-nineties trying to interpret the so-called "East-Asian miracle." There are big disputes about the extent to which the East-Asian miracle shows that market liberalism works, particularly when you realize that one of these countries is China, with a highly controlled economy indeed. The Japanese have never run a purely free-market economy. Neither have the Koreans. On the other hand, Singapore, Hong Kong were swashbuckling free-market capitalism. So there were debates about the extent to which state intervention in the free market pushed forward the East-Asian miracle.

CD1 Track 34

Ex 3.2
In Part 2 of the extract, the professor goes on to discuss another factor. Listen to Part 2 and continue the notes.

Part 2

But nobody disagreed about one element of the East-Asian miracle, and that was investment in people. Country after country in East Asia, it was argued, had undertaken reasonably equitable investments in health care, education, and training of people in those countries. And it was argued that this was a major stimulus to industrialization in this area, that you could always hire a lot of people at low labor rates, but who were in reasonably good health, who were literate and who had reasonable skills. And that was a difference between East Asia and, for example, Africa and Latin America. Or a difference, for that matter, between East Asia and South Asia.

CD1 Track 35

Ex 4.1
Listen to this extract from Track 34. The main stressed syllables in this sentence are marked in bold.

..., that you could **always** hire a lot of people at **low** labor rates, but who were in reasonably good **health**, who were **literate** and who had reasonable **skills**.

Ex 4.2
Listen to the following sentence from Track 33.

The Japanese have never run a purely free-market economy. Neither have the Koreans.

CD1 Track 37

Ex 4.3
Listen to the extract and complete the sentences with two to seven words in each blank.

You need to pre-test the questionnaire. This is really important. Those of you, some of you, will be doing this for, you know, your dissertation. Some of you, I know, are collecting primary data. You need to pre-test the thing, because you're the researcher. You're very close to the subject. You know what you're talking about. But you've got to check that other people do as well. And if you want a statistically valid sample of a hundred or two hundred people, then you've got to make sure that you're collecting the data properly. And it's here that these pre-tests, or pilots, they're going to tell you whether it's going to work or not.

So make sure that you do pilots, and, you know, this can be half a dozen different people that you question. I mean, you'll soon find out whether you've got any potential … or any doubts about the length of the questionnaire, or the style of particular questions, or whether the sort of questions that you're asking are valid. You'll soon find out from that. So, piloting or pre-testing is really important.

Unit 5: Note-taking: Part 2

CD1 Track 38

Ex 2.4
Listen and continue the notes. Use symbols and abbreviations.

Extract 1
Purposes of education

Three very broad perspectives from Littlewood, on the purposes of education. One is a very traditional one: pass on value, knowledge, and culture. So that you see education as passing from the previous generation down to the next generation, the knowledge they will need. Another purpose of education is to prepare students as members of society. So you have needs, which you feel your society must fulfill and you view education as a vehicle for doing this. And that will influence how language is taught—we'll see how in a moment. And the third view, which is much more humanistic, a humanistic view of education, is where you see students as individual selves who must be developed. And the process of education as being developing the self; bringing out the individual's best characteristics, allowing them to learn and to fulfill their potential.

CD1 Track 39

Ex 2.5
Listen and continue the notes. Use symbols and abbreviations.

Extract 2
World economy

What you have to understand is that from the early 1970s onwards there was this primary boom and there were signs of inflation in the world economy. In 1971, America left the gold standard. The value of the dollar had been linked to the value of gold and suddenly the government decided to cut it free. It was effectively devalued. Remember, in 1970 the American economy made up about a third of the total product of the world economy. Today it's about 25 percent or even less than that, but then the dollar had an even greater influence on the world economy.

So before the 1970s we had fixed exchange rates, but from 1971 America devalued the dollar and the exchange rates floated. And from that moment onwards, the major industrial economies, which in the 50s and 60s had had inflation rates of one percent, two percent, three percent per year, suddenly found themselves with inflation rates running at 10 percent, 15 percent, 20 percent. None of you in this room will believe me, probably, when I tell you that in 1971 Britain's inflation rate was 25 percent, yes. I can hardly believe that as the words come out of my mouth, and I can remember the year very, very distinctly as I was living over there at the time.

CD1 Track 40

Ex 3.2
Listen to this extract from a lecture entitled *Health in the United States* and make notes. Work with a partner. One of you should take notes in a linear style, the other should make a mind map.

Health in the United States

Well, so much for the problems of health in the developing world.

What I'd like to do now is look at the health situation in the developed world, with particular reference to the United States. I think the situation can be summarized briefly like this: firstly, life expectancy—how long people are living—is increasing. Secondly, we're taking more and more drugs and as a result of this we are curing, or at least controlling, many illnesses. However, what we're not doing as well as we should is stopping people getting sick in the first place.

Let me just illustrate this point with some statistics.

I've said that life expectancy in the United States is increasing and that is true. For example, let's look at men aged between 35 and 74. The number of men in this age group who died dropped by about 30 percent between 1988 and 1998. Now that is a very large fall; 30 percent fewer deaths in this age group over a ten-year period. Now, it's clear to me that much of this fall has been due to the amount of drugs we take now to cure problems.

If we look at heart disease for example, and the drugs we take to regulate or "cure" it, we can see that the number of prescriptions issued by doctors has almost quadrupled—increased by just under 400 percent—in the last 20 years. This includes drugs to lower blood pressure and to reduce cholesterol. So we really are becoming a nation of pill takers but—and this is the point I want to emphasize—we are not attacking the underlying causes of heart disease. One major cause of heart disease is physical inactivity. And in the United States we are becoming more inactive; we're doing less physical exercise. If you look at the statistics on your handout, taken from *Transport Quarterly*, you will see these illustrate the percentage of trips by different travel modes around the world. For example, in the United States, 84 percent is by car, 1 percent by bike and 9 percent on foot, whereas in Holland, the same statistics are 45 percent, 30 percent and 18 percent. In other words, we are walking less than in other countries, we are cycling less than in other countries. So, more use of the car and less physical exercise is the overall picture.

Add to this inactivity an unhealthy diet and the results are disastrous. Look at the figures for obesity in the United States. The percentage of obese adults more than doubled between 1960 and 2000. So, as a nation we're becoming more obese as a result of poor diet and a lack of regular physical activity. And what does this mean in terms of life expectancy? Well, over 2 million people die every year as a result of heart disease. And about 20 percent of these deaths—so, more than 400,000 deaths—according to the National Center for Chronic Disease Prevention, are premature. In other words, people are dying earlier than they should.

So, here in the US we could do more. Other countries are already doing more. Norway, for instance, has witnessed a drop of 54 percent in the number of deaths in men aged between 35 and 74 in the last ten years of the 20th century. And, as we saw earlier, in that same age group, the US has a figure of 30 percent. So, although that seems good, we could and we should be doing more, and we should be looking at how to prevent heart disease rather than concentrating only on how to cure it.

Ex 4.1
Listen and complete the following sentences.

a) The government has introduced tax incentives to encourage investment in this region.

b) For tax purposes, these organizations are often regarded as charities.

c) A number of reforms to the tax system have been proposed.

CD1 Track 42

Ex 4.2
Read the explanation and listen to the examples.

add up
what are these?
the main objective

do anything
try out
no idea of it

next day
rapid growth

CD1 Track 43

Ex 4.3
Listen to the following phrases. Mark the phrases with the symbols from Ex 4.2.

a) they invested in property

b) it's an open market

c) it's due on Friday morning

d) free admission on Sundays

e) it shows as a white mark

CD1 Track 44

Ex 4.4
Listen and complete the text with two to five words in each blank. The missing expressions include examples of word boundaries that may cause you difficulties.

Real options

I'm going to go through the theory of real options and then I'm going to show you how they can be used to raise some money, particularly on property assets. Real options are a term that was coined ten or 15 years ago, when people began to realize that net present value isn't the only thing you should look at in valuing assets, that a number of assets in companies have a great deal of option value. And so the option theory that you've been looking at can also be applied to real assets instead of just financial assets. And that, in raising money, companies particularly have a lot more to offer from an option pricing perspective than they first thought. The idea on real options is that management is not just a passive participant, that management can take an active role in making and revising decisions that can lead on from unexpected market developments such as, for example, the price of oil has gone up from $45 a barrel to in excess of $80 a barrel over the last year. So if you were an oil producer this time last year, you would be taking a very different view on the market for oil. So the increase in oil prices has uncovered a stream of options that make oil producers a lot more valuable, and now you can bring oil fields back on stream that were not necessarily economic. So this is the kind of idea that when we're looking at a project, we're not just looking at a static cash flow, we're actually looking at a cash flow that can be subject to a lot of optionality in it.

Unit 6: Introducing New Terminology

CD2 Track 1

Ex 2.1
Listen to the extract and make notes on the extended example.

Embedded words

I've been doing some research on one particular problem that arises out of this and I'd like to use that as a kind of a peg to hang this issue on, to tell you a little bit about it and where we've been going with this. It's the problem sometimes called the problem of embedded words. So, when we hear a word of several syllables like *responsibility*, a word like *responsibility* invariably contains several smaller English words. So in the case of *responsibility* we have—you can see here—*response*, *sponsor*, you have *ability* at the end there, and *bill* in the middle there and there are a few others if you looked hard enough you'll find some more. But almost any word in the English language that has more than two syllables will invariably contain within it, packaged up inside it, smaller English words. Now, consider what the brain is faced with if somebody produces a sentence containing the word *responsibility*. If the brain wrongly segments *responsibility* into *response* and *ability*, the decoding of that sentence is going to go catastrophically wrong. You see the point I'm making. So when we hear *responsibility*, it's that word; it's not a combination of "response" and "ability."

CD2 Track 2

Ex 3.2
Listen to the extract and complete the table.

European Union regulations and directives

OK, so the two types of European law I want to talk to you about today are directives and regulations, and these are very different, both in the way they are introduced and also in their scope, in the sense that one of them is more concerned with more serious matters while the other is more concerned with minor technical matters. Anyway I'll return to this in a moment and give you more details and more examples, but before I do that, I want to remind you of some of the key players in the European Union, as far as law-making's concerned. You might remember—I hope you remember—that there is the European Commission, the Council of Ministers and the European Parliament, and all these have a role in law-making. The European Commission is a non-elected organization, which is responsible for the day-to-day running of the EU. You can think of it as a civil service, or the administrators if you like, also called the "bureaucrats of Brussels," which is where the Commission's based. Then you have the Council of Ministers, which consists of one minister from each of the member states, so these are ministers who are part of the government in their own countries. Do you remember this? Yes? No? But that's clear, yeah, it is? Good. And finally we have the European Parliament, which consists of 626 members who are elected in their own countries to work as full-time MEPs, that is Members of the European Parliament.

So, what roles do these organizations play in law-making and what's the difference between regulations and directives?

Well, first, regulations. So, regulations come either directly from the Commission or from the Council of Ministers and they tend to be concerned with pretty minor technical matters, for example, how much beef there needs to be in a beef sausage, for example or, how much real cream there has to be in ice-cream. But they are not all trivial or unimportant things. There are regulations about standards of security in EU passports, for example.

And these regulations come into force as soon as they are published in what is called the *Official Journal*. So in other words, on the same day that these regulations are published, people in all the member states have to observe them, unless, and this is very important, unless individual member states have opted out of that particular area covered by the regulation. Let me give you an example of what I mean by opting out. Both the UK and Ireland decided they wanted to keep control of the whole area of visas and political asylum so they opted out. They said we will not be covered by EU regulation about those issues, so that's fine. So that's regulations. Now what about directives? Well, there are two main differences. The first is that directives have to be accepted first by the Council of Ministers. The Commission cannot do this on its own and the European Parliament cannot do this on its own. Directives can only come from the Council of Ministers. And even then the directive doesn't become legally binding in any member state until the parliament of that state introduces domestic laws to give the directive effect. So, for example, the directive comes from the Council of Europe but it doesn't automatically become law in Britain, for example. It's only legally binding, it only has legal effect, when the British parliament passes a British law. So unlike the case with Federal Law in the United States, it is not true that Britain is governed by European laws—many people believe that to be the case but it is simply not true. There have to be British laws. Is that clear? I know it's a little complex.

CD2 Track 3

Ex 4.3
Listen to the extract and make notes on the professor's definitions of both terms.

Market dominance and monopoly

What do I mean by making the distinction between market dominance and monopoly? We all know what a monopoly is, don't we? It's a single-firm case where the firm is in sole control of a market, and it's protected by such high entry barriers that its position is not vulnerable to competition. It's very rare in the real world for such firms to be in that happy position of being a complete monopoly. In the real world, however, you very often find that you have an approximation to dominance. Now, I've got an example … just looking for something here. Oh, here we are. I undertook a study in the mid-80s and it was quite easy for me to find 22 markets. The period covered, by the way, was the mid-70s to mid-80s. It was quite easy to find a number of markets where the first firm had a share of 50 percent or above. In some cases much higher; closer to sort of 80 or 90 percent even. And the second largest firm, or firms, were only half or less of the size, in terms of market share, of the dominant firm. So, although in many cases in the real world, you don't have monopoly—you only find that usually in the case of natural monopoly—the notion of dominance, as I want to use it, is quite frequent. You do frequently find one firm with a very sizeable market share. As a rule of thumb, if you like, upwards of 50 percent of the market, sometimes even as high as 80 or 90 percent. And the second-largest firm, or firms, has a share perhaps under 10 percent, or a number of smaller firms all of whom have quite small market shares. Now, I therefore mean by dominance that sort of market structure. The size distribution of firms is highly skewed. You've got one firm in pretty much in command of the market but a number of other firms operating in the market in competition.

CD2 Track 4

Ex 5.1
Listen to the following pairs of sentences. What is the difference in the pronunciation of the bold words in each pair? What might explain this difference?

a) ● What time **does** the train leave?
  ● I'm not sure why he's late. He **does** know about the meeting.

b) ● **Some** researchers have taken a different approach.
  ● We've just got time for **some** questions.

c) ● It was heated to 300°F **for** ten minutes.
  ● There are arguments **for** and against GM crop trials.

d) ● I'm not sure what you're getting **at**.

● There were **at** least five errors in the program.

e) ● Increasingly, small memory devices **can** store large amounts of data.

● Well, I **can** do it, but I don't want to.

f) ● Oh, are they going to interview **us**, as well as the students?

● Can you tell **us** what you've found?

CD2 Track 5

Ex 5.3
Listen and complete the extract with three to five words in each blank. In each case, at least one of the missing words is a function word.

Multiple-choice questions—easy. They reduce interviewer bias; very easy for people to … very easy and fast for people to answer; very easy for data processing. But the argument goes that they are difficult to design. The thing about multiple-choice questions is that you are forcing people into certain answers. This is a good reason for piloting. If you have a multiple-choice question and you pilot it, you may find that people are not, they don't put the issue that you're asking them into that particular set of categories that you've imposed. So that's where your pilots and qualitative research will help. Let me just show you an example of this.

Unit 7: What Professors do in Lectures

CD2 Track 6

Ex 2.2
The professor talks about four methods of market research in this lecture. Listen and complete the notes on the four methods.

Doing market research

These are the four most common ways, not necessarily in order, but if you're thinking of how market researchers collect their information those are the ways they do it. Computers are being used to support market researchers a lot more and the whole business of both selling things over the phone and doing market research over the phone has become a very important issue in market research and you'll see reference to terms like CATI: computer-assisted telephone interviewing. I think it probably goes without saying now that when you get a call and somebody wants to conduct a market research interview with you, they're probably sitting in front of a PC and we'll look at some of the implications of that. But one of the main ones of course is that the data entry occurs at the same time as the asking of the questions so there's huge savings in terms of that and indeed some of the analysis can go on more or less as you're speaking; things like, you know, in questionnaires you'll need to need to skip from one section to another, well the computer does that automatically. Next week you're going to hear about a technique called adaptive conjoint analysis and this is an analysis method that, as it suggests, adapts to the person who's being interviewed and starts to react or ask different questions depending on the person.

Telephone interviewing is increasing in its coverage, its importance but in some ways it's mail questionnaires that we want to concentrate on today, because it's mail questionnaires that in a sense have to be the most accurate, because mail questionnaires are the ones where the respondent doesn't have any help at all. There may be follow-ups and you may follow up by phone and so on but it's mail questionnaires that need to be the most accurate.

Personal interviewing in some ways is very good; very high levels of response, because—although you might have told somebody on the street who is trying to hassle you to answer a few questions to go away—the response rate for personal interviews is actually far higher than these other methods.

People find it a lot more difficult to turn away somebody who's standing there in front of them. The problem with personal interviews of course is that the interviewer is there and the interviewer themselves can bias the results and I think it's a lesson in research in general that interviewer bias of course is to be avoided, but if you've got somebody in person and they say "Well how about … ?" or "Do you mean … ?" and this kind of thing and this is where distortions can come in. So, personal interviews are good—high response rates—but there's the problem of bias and of course they're very expensive, you're employing real people to ask these questions.

Telephone interviewing—less expensive but a less good response rate and again some problems of bias. There's a problem whenever you're a person who's asking another person questions. There's always a problem of bias because you want people to expand on their answers and you want people to chat about what they're interested in and therefore you have to interact with them and that interaction's what can cause the biases. The alternative is to have a very strict interviewing schedule and a very strict questionnaire and you do get this particularly on the phone where, you know, you get this automaton who's actually a person but they're … it's a very stilted kind of interview and some would say that the quality of the data that's collected as a result is not that high. So we're concentrating on mail questionnaires but accepting that you need a good data collection device.

CD2 Track 7

Ex 3.2
Listen to Part 1 of the extract on how the experiments were carried out. Complete the notes.

Social learning: Part 1

So it seems very plausible that monkeys in the wild learn to fear snakes from other monkeys who've already acquired the fear. And Mineka set up an experimental situation where observer monkeys could watch—who were of course naive and didn't fear snakes initially, as you'll see—could watch a demonstrator who previously had learned fear of snakes, for example, a wild caught monkey. And the question is: What would the observers learn from the demonstrator? To explain the procedure before I show you the data, the observers were tested three times. First of all a pre-test when they were still naive and they'd never seen a demonstrator acting afraid of snakes; a post-test immediately after they'd seen a demonstrator acting afraid of snakes; and then a follow-up three months later, with no intervening training, to see whether whatever they'd learned was persistent. And the way the observers were tested was in a choice circus, which was just a round arena with four objects at the four corners, one of which was a model snake, and the other three were neutral objects, and they simply measured how much time the observer monkey would spend near the snake. If they were not frightened of snakes they'd spend about a quarter of the time near the snake and a quarter of the time near the other objects. If they were afraid of the snake they'd spend very little time near the snake and much much more time near the other objects. So, how much time they spend near the snake is one measure of fear. The other measure of fear is that they used something called a Wisconsin Test Apparatus, which is an apparatus simply where monkeys have to reach over a gap to get food and if you put a frightening stimulus in a glass box in the gap, the monkeys will be reluctant to reach over it to get to the food. So in this test they put either a real snake or a toy snake in a glass box and looked to see how slow the observers were to reach over the snake to get a tempting piece of food. And the slower they were and the more disturbed their behaviour, the more frightened they were concluded to be of snakes. So the question is: How did the observers' behavior change as a function of watching the demonstrators?

CD2 Track 8

Ex 3.3
Listen to Part 2 of the extract and make notes on the results and the conclusion the speaker draws from the results.

Social learning: Part 2

What do the observers do? OK, here they are on the pre-test when they're not afraid of snakes at all, and as you can see they divide their time equally between the four stimuli. They show no avoidance of snakes at all at the pre-test. But at the post-test—when they've had an opportunity to watch an observer who is in the presence of a snake and acting frightened—now they behave not as frightened as the demonstrator monkey, but very much more like the demonstrator. They spend a lot of time near the neutral stimulus and very little time near the snakes. So they've acquired a fear of snakes just by watching another monkey. And this fear is just as strong at the three-month follow-up as it was immediately after. So this is evidence that naive rhesus monkeys who are not afraid of snakes initially can learn that snakes are dangerous just by watching another monkey. They don't have to be bitten by a snake or attacked by a snake or anything, they can just learn it by watching another monkey.

CD2 Track 9

Ex 4.2
Listen to the extract and complete the notes.

Contestable markets

Essentially, what the theory predicts is that if an incumbent firm in such a market tries to raise its price above marginal cost, an entrant can immediately appear, undercut that price so long as it's in excess of the marginal cost, and still make a profit. So, if the incumbent firm responds and drops its own price to marginal cost, then the new firm, having made a profit previously, can then leave costlessly. The knowledge on the part of the incumbent firm that that is the case—that if it tries to raise its price, or if there are two or three incumbent firms if they try to raise their price, it would immediately provoke entry and the price would then sink to marginal cost—will mean that the incumbent firms will be unable to raise their price above marginal cost. The significance therefore of the notion of perfectly free entry and exit, you can see—well, I hope you can—it's significant that here was a theory that was saying even if you've got very highly concentrated oligopolies, if these conditions hold, then you needn't worry; there are very few policies you need to adopt towards such industries because they will produce a performance that is in line with that of a perfectly competitive market.

My critique, or the critique of others as well, about the theory of perfect contestability is that if you change the assumptions slightly, the predictions change dramatically. It's very unstable. Let me give you an example of how ... of what I mean by that. If a particular market, for example, which a number of people have said is contestable, if there are inevitable delays between a firm announcing it's coming into the market and actually managing to produce—and if in coming into the market the entrant has to incur some sunk costs—they can only be slight sunk costs. So if there's a delay, a slight delay, between the firm saying I will come into the market, the firm has to build up capacity, there's a delay between the announcement and the actual production, and also if there are some slight exit costs—sunk costs—that the firm has to incur to come into the market, then the predictions of the model are dramatically different. An incumbent firm in such a market can charge the monopoly price, or if it's two or three firms they can charge near the monopoly price. They can charge near the monopoly price until the entrant appears. They can then immediately drop their price to the marginal cost. The entrant, having finally come in to production, would then make no money, in fact it would make a loss, it would make a loss equal to its sunk costs. If the entrant is aware of that, it would not come into the market. So the sequence is this, that, with slight alterations, if the notion of a perfectly contestable market is not met, if you make slight changes to the assumptions, even though the market may be approximately contestable, it may make a dramatic difference in the prediction because it means that the incumbent firms will continually be able to charge something approaching a monopoly price. Entry will not occur because the entrants will say, I have to incur some slight sunk costs to get into this market, and I won't be able to recover them, and I won't make any money because as soon I appear and produce, the price will collapse to the marginal cost.

CD2 Track 10

Ex 5.2
Listen to the following short texts.

a) Earthquakes are a relatively rare occurrence in some parts of the world, and when they do occur, they are generally of such low magnitude that they are frequently not recognized as such.

b) Although hospital workers may be exposed to fairly low levels of radiation, measures need to be taken to keep exposure to a minimum.

c) Japan emerged from the postwar period with a developed electronics industry, and its emergence on the global consumer goods market gave US manufacturers strong competition.

d) It is widely assumed that poverty exists only in developing countries, but this assumption has meant the needs of the urban poor in developed countries are often neglected.

e) The particles collide at something near the speed of light and this collision releases massive amounts of energy.

f) A lot of time was spent trying to involve parents in the road safety plan, because previous experience has shown that the involvement of the local community in such projects is essential to their success.

g) Research has shown that male lions in different parts of Africa behave in different ways when faced with danger. Do environmental factors account for these differences in behavior?

h) We studied the performance of these financial products over a period of three years, and we found that some perform significantly better than others.

CD2 Track 11

Ex 5.3

Listen to the following short texts and complete them with words or phrases that are synonyms.

a) Many people are worried that young people lack strong role models, and this concern has prompted the police to question the conduct of professional athletes, whose actions may have a significant influence on young people.

b) The US decided to stay away from the Moscow Olympics in 1980, in protest at the Soviet Union's invasion of Afghanistan. Four years later, the Soviet Union retaliated with its own boycott of the Los Angeles Olympics.

c) Many multinational companies prefer to team up with local enterprises. Such alliances have a number of advantages.

d) The public's perception of the government's handling of the economy was critical. While the economy had in fact grown by two percent, people viewed the high unemployment rate and the government's inability to control strikes as indicators of poor performance.

Unit 8: Digressions

CD2 Track 12

Ex 2.2
Listen to the recording and read the extract. Then answer the questions.

My first set of examples come from a—oh, but first I'm going to talk about some fairly classic experiments in this lecture, but I would point out before I go on that there is a really excellent chapter on this subject in Shettleworth's book, which is referred to in the reference list for this lecture. Sara Shettleworth has a superb chapter on social learning. It's called "Learning from others." It's very up-to-date, very thoughtful, very comprehensive, and I'm just going to mention just a few of the examples that she mentions. But if you seriously want to think about this area, and it involves many complexities, her chapter is a very good place to go. Anyway, some of the best-known work on social learning, or putative social learning, in rats, in animals, are about food preferences. These are examples of learning the significance of stimuli, learning what foods are good to eat and what foods are bad to eat.

CD2 Track 13

Ex 3.1
Listen to Part 1 and make notes on the main points of the lecture. Do not make notes on the digression.

Part 1

Now, I'm going to show you lots of examples of different types of questions that you can ask. Here are some very general design issues though. Questions need to be precise, as you'll see in a moment. They need to be well-ordered. Incidentally—oh, I should have mentioned this earlier—the assessment for this course will, I think, be announced next week, formally, but what it's going to be is a case study. Basically you're going to be asked to evaluate, to comment, appraise. And it'll be a case study describing a typical market research process, but it will also include data. There will be data that you can analyze to support your case, and you will be able to analyze it, basically, in whatever way that you want. That'll be up to you. Somebody was asking earlier about will you have to do a questionnaire, and they've probably been talking to people last year who did it where everybody—basically every single individual—ran a questionnaire and it basically just got out of hand. It was extremely difficult to mark because people were producing huge volumes of stuff. But this session now is just basically to introduce you to how this sort of data is collected, but you won't be doing this as part of the assessment. So, your questions they need to be precise, and I'm going to show you some examples of good and bad questions in a moment. You need to decide very carefully, I think, on the ordering. I think there's really not an excuse for it these days, in a sense, for getting this part of it wrong and certainly presentation is very important so we'll talk a little bit about presentation and how you're able to order your questions to make sure that you get— well, there are different schools of thought, but—to make sure that you get an optimum response.

CD2 Track 14

Ex 4.1
Listen to Part 2 and make notes on the main points. Do not make notes on the digressions.

Part 2

So you've got to set very clear objectives as to what your questionnaire is designed to achieve. You need to say something about how you're going to collect the data, the kinds of question that you're going to have, the way that you word them, the flow of the questionnaire and so on. Obtaining approval is very important. In the university we have a body known as the Professional Standards and Ethics Committee. Technically speaking, if you go out, well if you go outside the university to research anything, you need to get the approval of the Committee. And the Professional Standards and Ethics Committee is, in many ways, a very good idea. The university, and really any market research body, that doesn't want its name muddied by the market research process, of course, and so we have to, if we're going out and indeed if students are doing projects, we have to get the implicit approval of the Committee. Sometimes that can come from the head of the department.

But two or three years ago, just for your information, this group was actually a group of undergraduate students, they decided to do a market research project that was part of the assessment for the course. And they were given a free choice as to what subject they wanted to ask people about. And the explicit instruction was that the people they researched should only be members of the class. And this group came and said we want to do a kind of a sex survey. And what this was, it was actually fairly innocent, although I did say, you know, this must be kept strictly within the group, and it, well, I won't go into the details, but it was asking various pretty personal questions really. And the next thing I heard, the next thing I heard of it, was somebody called up from—I can't remember where—but they'd actually been accosted by one of these students somewhere downtown and been asked these questions. And as you can imagine we got into a little bit of trouble about it, and we hadn't cleared it, I hadn't cleared it basically with the Committee, because it wasn't, I didn't believe it was going out—I didn't think it was going outside. So, anyway, there are, obviously very potential problems in that, but you do need to obtain approval. There is a market research society code of practice on asking questions, on how to do research.

You need to pre-test the questionnaire. This is really important. Those of you, some of you, will be doing this for your dissertation. Some of you, I know, are collecting primary data. You need to pre-test the thing, because you're the researcher. You're very close to the subject. You know what you're talking about. But you've got to check that other people do as well. And if you want a statistically valid sample of a hundred or two hundred people, then you've got to make sure that you're collecting the data properly. And it's here that these pre-tests, or pilots, they're going to tell you whether it's going to work or not.

So make sure that you do pilots and, you know, this can be half a dozen different people that you question. I mean you'll soon find out whether you've got any potential … or any doubts about the length of the questionnaire or the style of particular questions, or whether the sort of questions that you're asking are valid. You'll soon find out from that. So, piloting or pre-testing is really important.

CD2 Track 15

Ex 5.2
Listen and make notes on the main points. The four points in the introduction to this task will help you. Do not make notes on the digression.

Now here's an idea out of the seventies, IRD, integrated rural development. This was the idea that when you worked in rural areas with the poor, and the smallholder and so on, what you tried to do was deliver a package of assistance across the sectors, on the grounds this would give you synergy.

Now just to give you a fairly exaggerated example, if you're trying to get people to plant new varieties of rice and use fertilizer to increase their yields, which you hope is a scale neutral technology that can be used by smallholders, then why not at the same time combat malaria, inoculate people against disease, clean up the water supply? Because all of those will give you better health, which is a good thing in itself but, of course, healthier farmers can work harder in the fields and so that complements the agricultural measures. And while we're at it, we're going to build some new access roads, because that will improve price relatives at the farm gate and reduce isolation. And while we're at it, we'll run an adult literacy campaign, because literate farmers can read the labels on fertilizer packs, and so on and so forth.

So there was the idea that you should try and do things in development in an integrated fashion across all sectors, because you get synergy, and you get more than the sum of the parts going on. Now integrated rural development was very, very exciting to work in. You got all kinds of things to try, and you've got quite a lot of resources to play with, but these resources were limited compared with needs. So what happened with integrated rural development was within any country, what you did was you took a country, and a country might look just like that, and it might have its capital there, and you take a country that looks just like that, and you do integrated rural development and you do it there, there, there, there, there, oh, and there. And yes, that is to scale yes, that is to scale. In other words, you get these little enclaves of very small areas, where donors are putting in resources and everything is done.

And in the early 1970s Kenya had six small integrated rural development programs, which were very very well documented and some contemporary, very influential thinkers about development worked on those projects in the early 1970s. But look how tiny they are. That really is to scale. These things were in very small areas indeed. Why? Because, although you could target resources for a small area, you couldn't have the whole country running the kind of programs that were run there. So because you did everything in integrated rural development, you could only do it on a small scale, concentrated in particular areas.

Now those six small experiences, I think, were all successes. They were successes, but I think, with the benefit of hindsight, we would have to say they were unrepeatable and institutionally unsustainable. When the donors got bored, and the funds ran out, and the foreign experts' contracts ended, and the Jeeps began to rust, these projects essentially stopped. Indeed, I arrived in this part of Kenya in 1979, which had been the administrative headquarters, and there were two or three file cabinets filled with files in my room. And I left them there for a while, and then one day I thought, what on Earth? And I went through these file cabinets, and it was all the stuff on four or five years, ten years earlier, of the implementation of this. Minutes, plans, documents, contracts, budgets, semi-annual reports, monthly reports, all this kind of stuff. And I looked at this, and I said, my goodness, this is a vital piece of development history here, but it's clogging up my office. So it all went out with the trash. There's never, never enough historians around to document these experiences, and that's the way. And as I threw them into the trash, I thought, well there you go, good idea at the time, good people working on it, quite a success, but not sustainable.

CD2 Track 16

Ex 6.1
Extract 1
Listen and complete the notes.

I think that realism excludes the possibility—and it's a growing one—that states can simply isolate themselves from the outside world. The growth of television, the growth of mass communications, have meant that it's virtually impossible for states to ignore what is going on around them, and public opinion has become more important in some respects within states, forcing states to do things that they might not otherwise do. So the strict application of power in terms of maintaining the hierarchy, of ignoring the interests of others, is simply slowly being withered away.

CD2 Track 17

Ex 6.3
Extract 2
Listen and complete the notes.

… ten years later, therefore, we have the Scandinavian ideas impacting on American office design. Another illustration of that might be, you'll discover in the course of the lecture, that some of the factors that are driving the unusual, sometimes, configuration of office buildings, not always but sometimes, have to do with employment legislation; workers' councils, employers' rights, employees' rights.

CD2 Track 18

Ex 6.5
Extract 3
Listen and complete the notes.

Nineteen eighty-two. None of the commercial banks gave any money to the developing world for the best part of ten years after the '82 debt crisis. They got such a bad fright by the debt crisis they more or less ceased lending to the developing world. So the only people who were lending money to governments in the developing world from 1982 onwards were other governments, other aid agencies, and other multilateral agencies like the IMF and the World Bank.